Rules on Paper, Rules in Practice

DIRECTIONS IN DEVELOPMENT
Public Sector Governance

Rules on Paper, Rules in Practice

*Enforcing Laws and Policies in
the Middle East and North Africa*

Edouard Al-Dahdah, Cristina Corduneanu-Huci, Gael Raballand, Ernest Sergenti,
and Myriam Ababsa

WORLD BANK GROUP

Contents

Boxes

Figures

Map

Tables

Foreword

On the morning of December 17, 2010, Tunisian street vendor Mohammed Bouazizi set up his fruit cart in the city of Sidi Bouzid. Hours later, a local police officer confiscated his goods, on the basis that selling them on the street was illegal. The officer also reportedly harassed Bouazizi in a humiliating public scene. The young vendor proceeded to the local government's office to complain. Then, his grievance unheard, he set himself ablaze in an act of ultimate despair. Bouazizi's sister best captured the reason of his predicament: "In Sidi Bouzid, those with no connections and no money for bribes are humiliated and insulted and not allowed to live."

This dramatic scene constituted a pivotal moment in the modern history of the Middle East and North Africa. The story resonated beyond Sidi Bouzid and Tunisia, sending shockwaves across the Arab World. Beyond the disputed legality of selling goods on the street, the vendor's desperate gesture illustrates how the relationship between enforcement authorities and citizens is often colored by socioeconomic background. The uneven implementation of the law, on the basis of a citizen's identity—in this case, poor, unemployed, unconnected—is at the heart of a larger problem of inequality.

Five years have gone by since Bouazizi's immolation, and the rule of law remains elusive in many parts of the Middle East and North Africa. The unguarded optimism that greeted the Arab uprisings has since given way to a sobering call for nuancing our understanding of the causal mechanisms that led to these uprisings, and ultimately our approaches to future reform. This book aims to refine our understanding of the rule of law by analyzing legal and policy outcomes not simply as a result of de jure standards and organizational capacity, but mainly as a practice embedded in political and economic incentive structures. It shows how the line between de jure standards and de facto application of law is permeable and can be manipulated by political and economic interests.

The volume examines three cases from the Middle East and North Africa that extend the application of the concept of rule of law beyond its traditional home of legal and judiciary reform and into core economic sectors: taxation in Morocco, customs in Tunisia, and land inheritance in Jordan. Each case carries economic consequences on the macro scale, and each has implications for social justice. In Morocco, the study finds that tax obligations may be renegotiated between influential taxpayers and the administration. In Tunisia, despite a decade of acclaimed legal and regulatory reforms for customs law, corruption and discretion remain rampant. In Jordan, women are being denied their right to property, enshrined in laws drawing on the Islamic Sharia, due to social pressure to relinquish these rights in favor of male relatives.

This study provides a wider theoretical lens, reinforced with empirical evidence, which provides a tool for policy makers to identify factors that may further or hinder the effective implementation of laws and regulations. At stake in understanding the process behind rule-of-law outcomes more deeply is the formulation of more nuanced and context-specific reform alternatives for enhanced social justice, economic growth, and political stability.

Shantayanan Devarajan
Chief Economist,
Middle East and North Africa Region

Acknowledgments

This book is a product of the Global Governance Practice and the Middle East and North Africa region of the World Bank. The project began under the close supervision of Guenter Heidenhof, Sector Manager, who inspired the team to think about the rule of law in the Middle East and North Africa in the wake of the first Arab uprisings, and Manuela Ferro, Sector Director, who provided ongoing encouragement. It continued under the guidance of Shantayanan Devarajan, Chief Economist for the Middle East and North Africa Vice-Presidency, James Brumby, Director, Global Governance, and Hisham Waly, Practice Manager.

The book is a collective effort by a small team led by Edouard Al-Dahdah and consisting of Cristina Corduneanu Huci (Central European University, Budapest), Gael Raballand, Myriam Ababsa (Institut Français du Proche-Orient, Amman), and Ernest Sergenti. Chapter 1 was authored by Cristina Corduneanu Huci and Ernest Sergenti, with inputs from Anya Vodopyanov. Ernest Sergenti was also responsible for the empirical work in chapter 2 and appendix A. Alejandro Ponce of the World Justice Project generously shared his most recent datasets and provided advice on the empirical analysis throughout. Cristina Corduneanu Huci authored chapter 3, the case study on taxation policy in Morocco. Gael Raballand wrote chapter 4, the second case study, on customs in Tunisia, with Caroline Duclos with background inputs from Mohamed Benkirane. Myriam Ababsa wrote chapter 5, on land regimes and women's inheritance rights in Jordan, with input from Abeer Dababneh, Amal Haddadin, Husam Madanat, and Eva Abu Halaweh, and editing by Alexander Peter. Patrick Barbieri applied his able language editing skills, and Seraphine Nsabimana provided administrative support to the team. The manuscript was published thanks to a grant from the Nordic Trust Fund for Human Rights at the World Bank, managed by Anders Zeijlon with Anna Autio.

At various stages of its preparation, the chapters benefited from the advice, peer-review, and encouragement of many World Bank colleagues, among them the late Ed Campos, and including Phil Keefer, Nick Manning, Lisa Bhansali, Paul Prettitore, Bernard Funck, Ann Brockmeyer, Bob Rijkers, Sarah Mousa, Verena Fritz, and Ellen Hamilton. The team is also thankful to Melani Cammett of Harvard University and Thomas Carothers of the Carnegie Endowment for International Peace for insightful conversations at an early stage of the project.

The team warmly thanks all those who contributed to this effort, including government officials and members of civil society from Morocco, Jordan, and Tunisia who contributed data and information, as well as any colleagues inadvertently not mentioned, but it bears full responsibility for any errors in the final version of this work.

About the Authors

Edouard Al-Dahdah is a Senior Public Sector Specialist at the World Bank. He worked at the World Bank Institute and the Middle East and North Africa region. He is a co-author of the upcoming World Development Report 2017 on Governance and the Law, and of *Better Governance for Development in the Middle East and North Africa* (2003). His fields of interest include economic history, the political economy of development, and governance empirics. He did his graduate work at the University of Chicago and Georgetown University, and his undergraduate work at the American University of Beirut.

Cristina Corduneanu-Huci is an Assistant Professor in the School of Public Policy at the Central European University, Budapest. She holds a PhD in Political Science from Duke University. Her research focuses on the political economy of nondemocratic regimes, development policies, state capacity, and government transparency. Her work has appeared in Comparative Sociology, the World Bank Policy Research Working Papers series, and several edited volumes. She is the co-author of *Understanding Policy Change: How to Apply Political Economy Concepts in Practice*, a book that explores the complex relationship between politics and economic development.

Gaël Raballand is a senior public sector and governance specialist at the World Bank. He holds a PhD in economics from Sorbonne University and a degree in political science and international public law. He co-authored four World Bank books on transport and trade in Africa and has also been involved in several customs reforms in Sub-Saharan Africa and North Africa.

Ernest Sergenti worked as a consultant at the World Bank in the Middle East and North Africa (MENA) and South Asia regions. Prior to that, Ernest was a Harvard-MIT Data Center Research Fellow and Statistical Consultant at Harvard University's Institute for Quantitative Social Science. He holds a PhD in Political Science with concentrations in Political Economy and Econometrics from New York University, and a Master of Science in Economics from the London School of Economics. Ernest is a co-author of several publications on political party competition, economic growth, and ethnic violence and civil war, including articles published in the *Journal of Political Economy* and *American Journal of Political Science*.

Myriam Ababsa is a social geographer who has been based in Jordan since 2000. She holds a PhD in Geography from the University François Rabelais of Tours. She was a researcher at the French Institute for the Near-East, where she directed the "Atlas of Jordan: History, Territories and Societies". Her work focuses on the impact of public policies on regional and urban development in Jordan and the Syrian Arab Republic. She researches governance, public participation in housing policies, and services delivery. She is the author of « Amman de pierre et de paix » (Paris: Autrement, 2007), « Raqqa, territoires et pratiques sociales d'une ville syrienne » (Beirut: IFPO, 2009). She has co-edited "Cities, UrbanPractices and Nation Building in Jordan" (Beirut: IFPO, 2011) and "Popular Housing and Urban Land Tenure in the Middle East" (University of Cairo Press, 2012).

Abbreviations

AEO	Authorized Economic Operator
CDC	Cour des Comptes/Court of Accounts
CGEM	Confédération Générale des Entreprises Marocaines
CGI	Code Général des Impôts/General Code of Taxation
CPA	Coalition Provisional Authority
DGI	Directorat Général des Impôts/Tax administration
DRI	Directions Régionales des Impôts/Regional Tax Administration
EAP	East Asia and Pacific
ECA	Eastern Europe and Central Asia
EESF	L'Examen de l'Ensemble de la Situation Fiscale
EPA	Environment Protection Agency
ESC	Economic and Social Council/Le Conseil Economique et Social
EU	European Union
FNPI	National Federation of Real Estate Developers
GCC	Gulf Cooperation Council
GDCL	Direction Générale des Collectivités Locales
GDP	gross domestic product
GNI	gross national income
IAM	*"Maroc Télécom"*
IGR	*Impôt Général sur le Revenu*
IR	*Impôts sur le Revenu*
IS	*Impôts sur les Sociétés*
LAC	Latin America and the Caribbean
LAR	Livre d'assiette et de recouvrement
LPF	Livre des Procédures Fiscales/Code of Fiscal Procedures
LPI	Logistics Performance Index
MAD	Moroccan dirham
PEFA	Public Expenditure and Financial Accountability
PJD	Parti de la Justice et du Developpement

QoG	Quality of Government
SCID	Studies in Comparative International Development
SIT	Tax information system
SSA	Sub-Saharan Africa
TGR	Trésorerie Générale du Royaume/General Treasury of the Kingdom
TND	Tunisian dinars
TRC	Tax Recovery Code/Code du Recouvrement
VAT	value added tax
WCO	World Customs Organization
WJP	World Justice Project
WTO	World Trade Organization

Overview

Introduction

In early 2011, the citizens of countries across the Middle East and North Africa (MENA) took to the streets to demand change in an enduring movement unprecedented in its scope and momentum. Protesters sought more opportunities to participate in governance, including the right to representation, assembly, public debate, and legal recourse. They also demanded equitable treatment by their governments, access to decent jobs and reliable public services. Most importantly, they forcefully demanded an end to undue economic privilege, discrimination at the hands of bureaucrats, and asymmetries in business opportunities.

Aspirations for greater economic opportunities, political freedoms, and social equality steeply raised the bar for Middle East and North Africa policy makers. At the same time, most governments in the region, including those that have come to power in recent political transitions, have been either unable or unwilling to satisfy these aspirations effectively, owing to a combination of growing economic and demographic pressure, perverse political incentives, rents, security threats, and geopolitical interests.

Four years later, in spite of these governments' failures to meet the initial hopes the Arab Spring unleashed, equitable treatment under the law and procedural fairness, both key features of the rule of law in its day-to-day manifestations, remain central to a broader conversation about the promises of rising popular expectations and the perils of not fulfilling them.

The rule of law is a theoretical concept social scientists use to describe a political order where laws are predictable and applied *equally* to all citizens, regardless of their political or economic influence.[1] Under the rule of law, no individual or group stands above the law. Laws "tie the hands" of even the most powerful citizens, including those charged with making and enforcing these same laws. The rule of law is an ideal. Few societies have achieved it completely, but some have come much closer than others. Nascent democracies and authoritarian regimes are especially far from the ideal. In such contexts, laws are either not clearly codified or, more commonly, they are applied selectively in accordance with private economic and political interests.

The primary focus of this book is on one key process that defines the rule of law: the practical enforcement of laws and policies, or the failure to do so. Are there significant and persistent differences in implementation across countries? Why are some laws and policies more systematically enforced than others? Are "good" laws likely to be enacted and, if not, what stands in the way?

Our goal is to attempt to answer these questions using both a theoretical framework and detailed empirical data. We take the view that the problem is not in flawed legal design or a country's specific "culture," but rather in the structure of *political and economic incentives*. In line with a large and growing body of literature, we argue that if a law or regulation has the potential to threaten powerful political or economic interests it may never be passed into law in the first place or, if it is, it may not be properly implemented or effectively enforced. Conversely, if a law or regulation offers concrete benefits to key political stakeholders, it is more likely to be systematically enforced. Our main contribution to the literature is in demonstrating not just *whether*, but *how*, powerful interests affect implementation outcomes.

The general argument, which echoes throughout the chapters, is that the drafting and implementation of laws and regulations that are compatible with principles of the rule of law depend on the incentives both lawmakers and implementing agencies have. If laws and their enforcement align with the goals of the ruling elites, effective implementation is a far more likely outcome. The incentives elites have to build and support rule-of-law institutions themselves derive from the distribution of power, especially the number and the relative strength of competing political interests in society. A society's power structure is partly a historical given. The point we endeavor to make, however, is that it is not deterministic. Realigning the *incentive structures* for reform among key actors and organizations can dramatically improve the chances that rule-of-law institutions will take root. On the other hand, building the capacity of organizations without first changing institutional incentives is likely to lead to perverse outcomes, with the capacity ultimately channeled toward goals the reformers never envisioned.

What Is the Rule of Law?

The concept of the rule of law is not new. It has appeared in various guises in writings for centuries, but it became popularized in the modern social sciences in the 1960s when progressive movements for social justice placed the law at the core of broad societal change by way of public interest litigation and legal aid to disadvantaged constituencies. A decade later, the third wave of democratization induced similar ideas among academics and policy makers interested in political reform and good governance in developing and transitioning countries. For many years the literature on the concept of the rule of law remained vague about its meaning (Kleinfeld 2012, 7). Some early studies simply discussed it in terms of the organizational characteristics deemed necessary for a modern legal order, usually the judiciary. For these studies, to promote the rule of law meant to strengthen the capacity of institutions by constructing and repairing courthouses, procuring furniture and equipment for the judiciary, training lawyers and judges, and organizing bar associations (Golub 2006, 109).

Following this "organizations-based" approach, experts and donors channeled large amounts of resources to programs aimed at strengthening the organizational capacities of courts and judiciaries. Two decades later, most experts agreed that these projects had failed to deliver improved rule of law in recipient countries (Golub 2006; Hammergren 2007). As we argue later over the course of this book, this failure was largely the result of a fundamental misunderstanding of what factors really shape the rule of law and what the main challenges to it are.

A second wave of studies focused on the ultimate *ends or outcomes* of the rule of law. According to this ends-based definition, states based on the rule of law have several characteristics in common. Their governments are subject to laws and they have set procedures for making new laws and policies. Their citizens are equal before the law and policy decisions are regulated by established procedures rather than the whims of individuals. Their citizens enjoy equal access to justice and effective dispute-resolution mechanisms. Human rights are legally protected and are enforced, and law and order prevail (Kleinfeld 2012, 14–15). This conceptualization is also in line with that of political philosophers who have debated the issues of limited government and equity before the law for centuries. It is the definition we use in this book.

Unlike the organizations-based approach, the ends-based approach provides a useful standard for judging the quality of laws and their implementation. What it cannot do is explain exactly why good laws and policies are adopted by some governments but not others, and why the implementation of laws varies so widely across countries and even within the same country.

Some scholars also distinguish between "thick" and "thin" definitions of the rule of law (Trebilcock and Daniels 2008). With thick definitions, rule of law is viewed as the backbone of a just and open society. Thin definitions of the rule of law, by contrast, focus more on specific laws and institutions, as well as their beneficial effects on economic outcomes. According to this definition, rules do not necessarily have to be just or promote open access. They have a beneficial impact because they regulate human interactions and thereby promote social cohesion. Property rights are a prime example.

We believe that the best way to understand the variation in the drafting and implementation of laws and policies is to look at the interests and incentives of those responsible for these tasks. Politicians do not adopt laws and policies that jeopardize their interests or the interests of their associates, but they will adopt and systematically enforce legislation as long as they have an economic or political incentive for doing so.

Constraints to the Rule of Law

How does rule of law evolve in the first place? Is it an accident of history or a deliberate political choice? The short answer is that it is both. Two groups in society have the power to create rules that produce socially desirable outcomes: (a) those responsible for formulating, revising, and interpreting laws—the executive, legislature, and the judiciary; and (b) those responsible for implementing the laws, regulating industries and organizations, and setting standards—the bureaucracy.

Two factors that determine the willingness of these two groups to promote outcomes that enhance social welfare: (a) the number of competing interests, individuals, and organizations in positions of influence, and (b) the relative balance of power among them. In general, wherever the number of competing interests is higher and power is more evenly distributed there is likely to be stronger rule-of-law institutions. Both competition and the balance of power are partly shaped by history, but they can also change over time through external shocks, including donor interventions aimed at institutional reform.

In autocratic regimes, the number of competing groups and interests with access to political or economic resources is small. The core of an authoritarian regime, made up of the autocrat and his associates, remains largely unchallenged, notwithstanding periodic elections, which the leadership rarely fails to win. As Maravall and Przeworski (2003, 4) note, "the difference between rule by law and rule of law lies then in the distribution of power, the dispersion of material resources, the multiplication of organized interests; in societies that approximate the rule of law, no group becomes so strong as to dominate the others." In autocracies where one political force monopolizes power and rules without restraint, there is no rule of law, but only the inferior rule by law, because, at most, law is an instrument of the dictator who, "by definition of sovereignty, is not bound by it" (Maravall and Przeworski 2003, 3).

The rule of law emerges only when there is competition: self-interested rulers willingly restrain themselves through laws when (a) there are competing political actors that are forced to resort to the law to resolve their conflicts and (b) compliance with the law is the only credible way the sovereign can obtain the sustained, voluntary cooperation of social groups commanding valuable resources. A point similar to the one Maravall and Przeworski make is forcefully argued by North, Wallis, and Weingast (2009), and Kleinfeld (2012, 91), who uses the Magna Carta to illustrate it:

> The modern rule-of-law state is often seen as having its beginning at the moment that the English nobility forced the king to sign the Magna Carta. ... The core reform was ... creating a force that amassed enough power to balance the power of the monarchy.

The second and related challenge to building rule-of-law institutions is the asymmetrical powers of organized interests. On the one hand, it is true that "in no society is power dispersed equally among disassociated individuals [and] as a result no state, however liberal or democratic, treats all citizens equally before the law" (Holmes 2003, 21). On the other hand, power disparities in autocratic regimes are substantially greater as most genuine competition to the autocrat or his associates and supporters is nipped in the bud through either repression or co-optation.

Contribution of the Volume

Our work builds on the mainstream literature on the rule of law in several important ways but also goes beyond it. First, our focus on *processes*, including gaps between law and practice and the politics behind those gaps, consciously departs from the mainstream emphasis on *specific legal institutions* that promote the rule of law, such as the judiciary.[2] Legal institutions are undeniably important, but they may not be the only or even the most important element affecting the rule of law. As Carothers (2003, 8) notes: "[It] is by no means clear that courts are the essence of a rule-of-law system in a country. …The question of which [organizations] are most germane to the establishment of the rule of law in a country is actually quite complex and difficult."

Instead of limiting ourselves to a particular type of organization or a narrow legalistic approach to rule of law, we present a broader theory to explain how laws are made and implemented across different types of sectors and organizations. To accomplish this goal we focus on the key political and economic incentives that lead to the enforcement or nonenforcement of laws and policies.

Second, in a related way, our contribution broadens the field of inquiry to include a range of sectors beyond the judiciary and the police in a search for a more direct causal relationship between the rule of law and economic development outcomes. Aside from being good in its own right, for its protection from the excessive intrusion of the state in one's personal affairs or from violence at the hands of other citizens, the rule of law may also lead to better economic outcomes.

Although the link between the rule of law and growth is not especially strong—certain countries did enjoy growth in the short term even as the rule of law was weak—evidence exists to support the claim that, in general, the rule of law promotes economic development (Rodrik, Subramanian, and Trebbi 2004). Some of the most common mechanisms associated with the rule of law that can promote economic growth are: (a) the protection of property rights, (b) the reduction in levels of violence, (c) institutional checks on government, and (d) lower incentives to distort public policy, through corruption (Haggard and Tiede 2011).

We take this discussion of the rule of law one step further and examine parts of the state not normally treated by rule-of-law scholars, for example, the tax and customs administrations, as well as other bureaucratic agencies that are causally closer to economic outcomes than courts and police agencies. In all these areas we look at both the presence of required laws and the quality of implementation. In the case of the tax and customs administrations, for instance, we analyze both differences in tax and customs laws across countries and differences in the ways, or degrees to which, existing laws are circumvented by powerful and influential individuals to the detriment of the many.

A final goal of this book is to provide tentative lessons for development practitioners working in the MENA region and perhaps other developing regions as well, regarding (a) the types of interests that can hamper the drafting and implementation of good laws and policies in given fields or sectors, and consequently potential pitfalls to avoid when designing and implementing costly new programs; and (b) which tangible governance reform strategies are more likely to work and have the greatest possible impact on the work of sector specialists. Although we recognize that challenges to the rule of law will differ from country to country and sector to sector, we believe that our in-depth comparative analyses of institutions and incentive structures speak to many settings beyond the sectors and countries analyzed in this volume.

Structure of the Volume

We begin by developing a theoretical framework in chapter 1, which brings institutions and the incentives they generate to the forefront of the discussion on the rule of law, rather than focusing on *organizational* capacity. In chapter 2, we present four hypotheses on how political economy factors affect rule-of-law outcomes, and provide empirical support for them using data from the Rule of Law Index of the World Justice Project and from the Global Integrity Index. We also compare rule-of-law outcomes for the MENA region with other countries of the developing world, and empirically examine the extent to which rule-of-law outcomes differ from formal written laws in MENA and other regions. We find that all developing regions present an "implementation gap," and that, on average, MENA is no different from other developing regions. Chapters 1 and 2 also serve as the respective conceptual and empirical foundations for a series of case studies, which highlight the policy implications for addressing rule-of-law challenges in different countries and bureaucratic agencies in MENA. This first volume features three case studies in three different bureaucratic agencies, on tax in Morocco (chapter 3), customs in Tunisia (chapter 4), and land in Jordan (chapter 5). More case studies will follow in a subsequent volume.

The three case studies in this volume look at these implementing units, their administrative capacity, and, most importantly, the incentives which agents in these organizations face within the surrounding political and social landscape. The choice of these bureaucratic agencies was primarily motivated by an intellectual desire to apply the concept of the rule of law beyond the boundaries development practitioners have hitherto confined it within, and place it squarely in the economic sphere. The selection of the cases was also driven by the emphasis the book chose to put on the problem of the enforcement of rules and regulations, the collection of taxes and the levying of custom duties being the domains where government authority is enforced *par excellence*.

The first case, in chapter 3, examines the implementation gap between tax policy and practice in Morocco, tests hypotheses with respect to its political economic causes and explores two main findings. *First*, the border between law and implementation is permeable, leaving room for "individualized" renegotiation of tax obligations between influential taxpayers and the administration.

The broad range of tax exemptions, the use of fiscal amnesties, and the stock of tax arrears have had negative consequences on perceptions of equity and fairness. *Second*, lobbying claims as well as the need to deploy low administrative capacity to collect revenue from the most taxable sectors are the most important political economic variable explaining unequal treatment of taxpayers at the micro-level.

Focusing on Tunisia, the second case, in chapter 4, shows that customs efficiency in Tunisia did not improve despite the adoption over the past decade of numerous legal and regulatory reforms in line with international standards. While trade facilitation may have improved—but not to the extent official data suggests—the fight against corruption has largely failed. The increase in fraud and smuggling is the result of discretionary behavior by customs agents and the selective implementation of rules. Political interference, the lack of accountability and rent-seeking behavior of some customs officers, and poor administrative traceability conspire to account for this growing gap between paper and practice.

The third case, in chapter 5, shows how norms and attitudes toward women in Jordan led to their de facto exclusion from property ownership. The right of women to inherit property—but not in equal shares with men—is enshrined in the Constitution, in Islamic Sharia, and even in customary law, yet in practice, female heirs continue to face social pressure to relinquish these rights in favor of their male relatives. Such pressure can take the form of intimidation and even physical violence. Softer methods to deprive women of their inheritance rights include donations by owners to male heirs prior to their death. In most cases, women receive a symbolic gift that is far from equivalent to the monetary value of the land or the apartment. The social stigma from contesting this trend is high, so few women go to court to fight for their rights. However, there has been progress recently. Social mobilization by women's rights activists did result in the amending of the Jordanian Personal Status Law, and the introduction of a number of articles on property and exclusion that credibly commit courts and bureaucratic enforcement agencies to protect the rights of women. Statistics and surveys tend to show a slight improvement in women's inheritance patterns in Jordan over the past 25 years. This is attributed to women's increased awareness of their rights, but also, ironically, to stronger religious conservatism, which encourages men to implement "God's law."

Notes

1. We ordinarily associate the rule of law ... with a roughly equal treatment of social groups." Holmes (2003, 21)
2. Carothers (2003, 8) notes that in the last 10 to 15 years the emphasis on judiciaries in the rule-of-law field has become so widespread that the terms *judicial reform* and *rule-of-law reform* are often used interchangeably. The reason for this, he explains, is that most specialists in the rule of law are lawyers who think of courts as the core institution of law enforcement.

References

Carothers, Thomas. 2003. *Promoting the Rule of Law Abroad: The Problem of Knowledge.* Washington, DC: Carnegie Endowment for International Peace.

Golub, Stephen. 2006. "A House without a Foundation." In *Promoting the Rule of Law Abroad: The Search for Knowledge,* edited by Thomas Carothers, 105–36. Washington, DC: Carnegie Endowment for International Peace.

Haggard, Stephan, and Lydia Tiede. 2011. "The Rule of Law and Economic Growth: Where Are We?" *World Development* 39 (5): 673–85.

Hammergren, Linn. 2007. *Envisioning Reform: Conceptual and Practical Obstacles to Improving Judicial Performance in Latin America.* State College: Pennsylvania State University Press.

Holmes, Stephen. 2003. "Lineages of the Rule of Law." In *Democracy and the Rule of Law,* edited by Jose Maria Maravall and Adam Przeworski, 19–61. Cambridge, UK: Cambridge University Press.

Kleinfeld, Rachel. 2012. *Advancing Rule of Law Reform Abroad: Next Generation Reform.* Washington, DC: Carnegie Endowment for International Peace.

Maravall, Jose Maria, and Adam Przeworski, eds. 2003. *Democracy and the Rule of Law.* Cambridge, UK: Cambridge University Press.

North, Douglass, John Wallis, and Barry Weingast. 2009. *Violence and Social Orders: A Conceptual Framework for Interpreting Recorded Human History.* Cambridge, UK: Cambridge University Press.

Rodrik, Dani, Arvind Subramanian, and Francesco Trebbi. 2004. "Institutions Rule: The Primacy of Institutions over Geography and Integration In Economic Development." *Journal of Economic Growth* 9 (2): 131–65.

Trebilcock, Michael J., and Ronald J. Daniels. 2008. *Rule of Law Reform and Development: Charting the Fragile Path to Progress.* Northhampton, MA: Edward Elgar.

CHAPTER 1

Theoretical Framework

Introduction

Several theoretical concerns drive this book's approach. Among these is the recognition that a large body of academic and policy work on the rule of law has emphasized the centrality of two assumptions in explaining rule-of-law outcomes: the quality of laws and the quality of legal interpretation. The focus on these two technical assumptions shaped donors' traditional solutions to the problem of policy failure: invest first in "good" laws on paper, and second, in an independent judiciary with the capacity and willingness to properly interpret the laws. Once these two elements were in place, the evident policy response to lagging legal equity became to attempt to close or at least reduce the "implementation gap" by boosting organizational capacity, while assuming recipients' "good" policy intentions along the way.

This book questions these two assumptions theoretically, and tests them empirically and analytically in the case of the Middle East and North Africa (MENA) region. It probes whether rule-of-law problems are serious and, if so, whether they indeed come from a technically imperfect translation from de jure to de facto. Rather than proposing a generic answer to this question, it puts politics in the mix and finds that an implementation gap that is uniform across sectors and laws should not be taken for granted: indeed, case studies in chapters 3, 4, and 5 illustrate how the magnitude of this gap varies widely from rule to rule and agency to agency depending on political incentives.

The book also turns the second assumption, on the centrality of legal interpretation, into an empirical question, and asks whether it is exclusively a story of judicial failure. Instead, it looks at bureaucratic performance as a primary site of rule of law or rule by law, and argues that it affects citizens more tangibly than the judiciary does. Good courts as venues for appeal are undeniably important, but access to justice for every citizen whom bureaucrats treat unfairly cannot be taken for granted. Appealing in court often entails costs prohibitive to the poor, excluding large segments of the population of many countries. The broad conceptualization of the rule of law in this volume and the focus on bureaucracies allows us to understand systemic inequities irrespective of the economic class to which their subjects belong.[1]

Without doubt, inequities and unfairness of treatment emerge when formal laws and regulations systematically favor some individuals or groups over others. Yet even when the political process corrects these formal forms of discrimination, inequities can and do persist because the implementation of laws and regulations systematically favors some individuals or groups over others, or because social norms undercut formal correctives. This persistence of unequal treatment motivates this book's quest to better understand when and how implementation goes right—guaranteeing everybody's fair treatment—and when and how it goes wrong—privileging cronies and narrow special interests over ordinary citizens. The institutional incentives of governments to properly enforce laws are at the heart of this quest.

The discipline of political economy provides useful tools for examining issues related to institutions and the incentives they generate. From a political economy perspective, institutions comprise *formal rules*, including laws, regulations, and policies; *norms* such as attitudes toward minorities and customs such as reciprocity and gift giving; and *enforcement mechanisms* that apply to both formal and informal rules, such as credible threats of penalties or ostracism (North 1990). All three parts of an institution mold behavior that ultimately leads to outcomes that matter for society: for example, whether citizens enjoy equal treatment before the law, whether human rights are respected, and whether law and order prevails. For formal laws to be sound, compatible with norms, and effectively and equitably enforced really depends on the incentives of political decision makers and those responsible for enforcement.

This first chapter sets out a general theoretical framework that considers the rule of law in the broader context of political institutions. It first bridges these two concepts, then briefly goes through a well-established theoretical framework many readers may already be familiar with. It then makes a case for putting the *rules of the game* at the forefront of the discussion on the rule of law, rather than focusing on *organizational* capacity. Finally, it proposes an analytical matrix intended to help policy makers decide when and under what conditions policy interventions are likely to pay off or not.

Institutions as Rules of the Game

To understand why institutions matter for the rule of law and how they shape the incentives and behavior of individuals, it is necessary to consider first what motivates individuals. The political, economic, and social systems of any modern society can for these purposes be viewed as a game in which individuals are the players; the rewards at stake are different kinds of material, political, social, psychological, or other goods; and players pick strategies to maximize the desired goods they receive. Politicians play the game of electoral and nonelectoral politics: they compete for votes among the electorate, for access to positions of power and influence, and for access to a top official's ear. Rank-and-file state employees, such as bureaucrats, tax collectors, and customs officials, compete for promotions and pay raises. Business owners compete for markets and profits, and by capturing greater market share, they drive out competitors. Members of social organizations, such as charities and religious groups, compete for membership, name recognition, contributions, and social impact. The behavior and strategies players adopt based on their incentives therefore shape the game.

The basic need to survive and informal institutions such as obligations to family, the smallest social and economic unit in a society, are the two main drivers of individuals' behavior. In the absence of any other incentives or constraints, their pursuit of gains will lead to outcomes that may be optimal for the strongest individuals or families but detrimental to others in society, and therefore conflict with socially desirable outcomes such as equality before the law and law and order. If there is nothing to counterbalance the selfish, the selfish will prevail. In the absence of antitrust laws, corporations will establish exclusive monopolies. Similarly, if there are no sanctions, ordinary citizens will lobby and bribe authorities to secure preferential tax relief or access to services. In short, in the absence of any institutions other than the family, the game individuals play in society will be zero-sum, geared to basic survival. Nothing would restrain selfish behavior and, taken to the extreme, society could approximate Thomas Hobbes's description of the state of nature, where life is "poor, nasty, brutish, and short."

Institutions of the rule of law, like all institutions, are "humanly devised constraints that shape human interaction" (North 1990, 3), or more simply, man-made rules of the game designed to realign individual incentives so that they are more compatible with socially desirable rule-of-law outcomes. Good laws and policies and their enforcement can make it in the people's interest to shun corruption, avoid monopolistic business practices, pay taxes, and seek services as a right rather than as a favor. A growing body of experimental evidence suggests that this change in behavior and in seemingly age-old practices can take place fast as people react and optimize their strategies based on new incentives (Abrams, Bertrand, and Mullainathan 2007; Berge and others 2015; Duflo, Fischer, and Chattopadhyay 2005).

All three parts of an institution— *formal rules, informal norms, and enforcement mechanisms*—have to be aligned for individual incentives to favor rule-of-law outcomes. Formal laws need to be in place for a clear understanding of which behaviors are acceptable and which are not, and a legal basis for law enforcement agencies to sanction offenders. Informal norms and customs need to be aligned with formal laws or, at the least, not contradict them. For their part, the agencies responsible for enforcement need to have both the will and the means to do so. For example, if a government intends taxation to be fair, citizens need to know that a formal law free of loopholes, such as exemptions for influential individuals, exists on the books; that personal connections or bribery will be of no use to them; and that enforcement will be evenhanded and entail a penalty should they fail to pay. If all three elements align, citizens would have the incentive to pay their taxes, because there would be no other alternative, and because the penalty for breaking the law would be costly.

Yet, more often than not, one part or the other of this trinity of the rule of law is missing. *Formal laws* might be undermined by loopholes that make them non-transparent and enshrine privileges of cronies or powerful interest groups. The case of taxation in Morocco analyzed in chapter 3 of this volume illustrates this problem. Chapter 4 shows that the internal incentives of the *enforcement* agency overseeing customs services in Tunisia significantly reduced the impact of technical reforms. Chapter 5 demonstrates how *informal norms* sometimes undermine strong laws regulating land ownership in Jordan and perpetuate de facto unequal or unfair treatment of women that laws on paper meant to abolish in the first place. The rule of law, in the sense of equity of treatment and procedural fairness for citizens and groups, is realized when all three pieces of the institutional trilogy—formal rules, informal norms, and enforcement mechanisms—come together harmoniously.

From Organizations to Institutions

Institutions shape behavior both directly and indirectly. In direct ways, they permit or proscribe one form of behavior or another. For example, laws stipulate which citizens are subject to which taxes, set speed limits on roads, and prescribe penalties for corruption. Institutions also influence behavior indirectly, through the organizations that govern individuals, or the organizations citizens join. Organizations, defined as "groups of individuals bound by some common purpose to achieve objectives" (North 1990, 5)—such as the tax collecting agencies that control who pays how much in tax, police agencies issuing speeding tickets, courts imposing fines and jail sentences on corrupt officials, or political parties and civic associations—are themselves created and shaped by institutions. Indeed, as figure 1.1 shows, organizations *are not* institutions, but rather conduits for the institutions, that affect individual incentives and behavior.

Organizations are omnipresent in modern societies. They can be political, economic, or social in nature, and they include the police, the courts, parliaments, political parties, trade unions, businesses, churches, and community associations. Human societies are structured around organizations because people find them useful in achieving shared political, economic, or social goals. They offer economies of scale, information shortcuts, and many other tangible benefits to their members. For instance, bureaucracies represent a cost-effective

Figure 1.1 Direct and Indirect Effects of Rule-of-Law Institutions on Individual Behavior

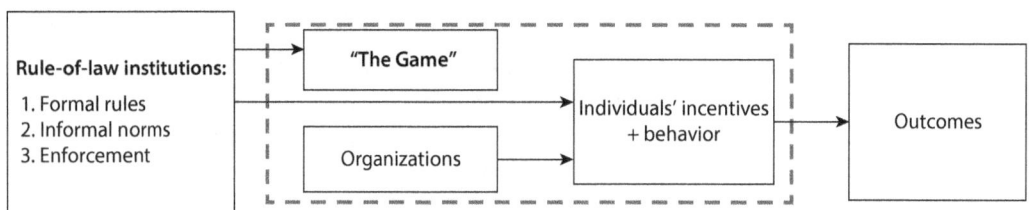

means for governments to coordinate the efforts of governing, while political parties act as informational shortcuts for voters as they evaluate the qualifications of competing politicians.[2] Box 1.1 describes the relations between institutions, whether political, economic or social, and state and non-state organizations and figure B1.1.1 illustrates it.

Box 1.1 "The Game": Political, Economic, and Social Systems

Inside the blue box are the players of the game: individuals and political, economic, and social organizations that compete to improve the welfare of individuals. Organizations are comprised of two sets: those that constitute the state,[a] such as the army, the executive, the courts, and the bureaucracy; and political, economic, and social organizations outside the state. State organizations are important in light of the power they wield over various social goods with a direct impact on people's lives. These include taxation, public services, the police, and the courts, among others. Many of the challenges to rule of law—and remedies—originate with these organizations.

Institutions, as combinations of formal rules, informal norms, and enforcement mechanisms, are represented by green ovals in figure B1.1.1. They fall outside the scope of the game, but have the power to shape it. Some institutions are created and modified by the state. Other institutions, however, such as some social norms, may be independent of the influence of the state. The outcomes of the game are listed in the gray box. In figure B1.1.1, the green arrows represent the effects that institutions have on individuals and organizations.

Political institutions create both state and nonstate political organizations and mandate what they do, how their leaders are selected, and what incentives the individuals who staff them have. Examples include constitutions and electoral systems. Constitutions delineate the organizations of the state, the executive, the legislature, and the judiciary, their powers and their relationships with each other. Electoral laws or systems regulate in greater detail how elections are conducted, for example, who is eligible to run for office and how votes are to be aggregated, and they establish regulatory organizations such as electoral commissions to monitor elections and enforce electoral laws.

Economic institutions regulate market transactions and activities. Among other things, financial laws and regulations govern the organization of banks and insurance companies; define the nature of the business transactions they are permitted to conduct; and set limits on foreign ownership of domestic industries. Environment regulations issued by a government agency such as the U.S. Environmental Protection Agency determine what types of emissions are deemed pollutants or whether a particular industry has violated an environmental law or regulation.

Social institutions are less formal. They can be comprised of no more than norms, and depending on the norm, perhaps an enforcement mechanism. In some societies, norms may forbid a woman from marrying without her family's consent, and when a woman violates these norms, her family may go so far as to kill her to protect the family's honor, an extreme enforcement mechanism. Other norms may bar women or certain ethnic minorities from certain occupations.

box continues next page

Rules on Paper, Rules in Practice • http://dx.doi.org/10.1596/978-1-4648-0886-9

Box 1.1 **"The Game": Political, Economic, and Social Systems** *(continued)*

Figure B1.1.1 "The Game": Political, Economic, and Social Systems

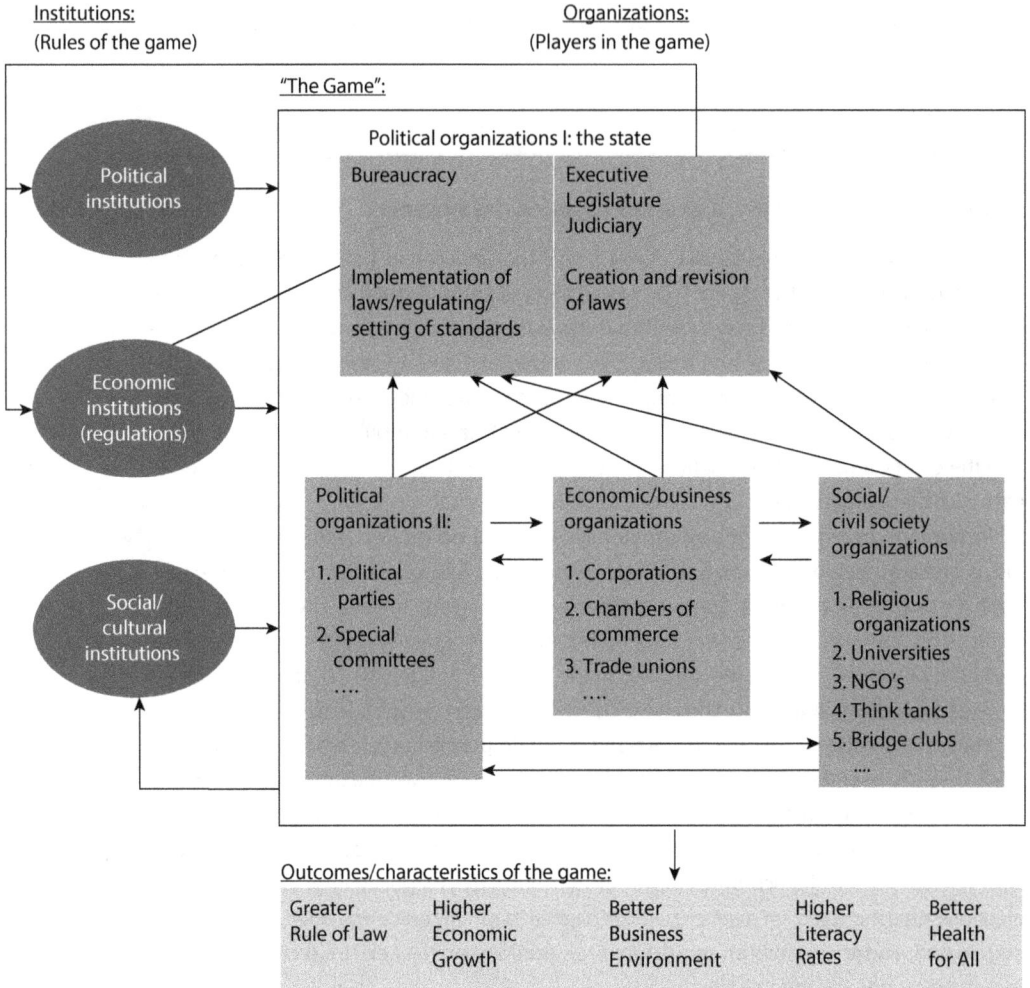

Institutions:
(Rules of the game)

Organizations:
(Players in the game)

"The Game":

Political organizations I: the state

Bureaucracy	Executive Legislature Judiciary
Implementation of laws/regulating/ setting of standards	Creation and revision of laws

Political institutions

Economic institutions (regulations)

Social/ cultural institutions

Political organizations II:

1. Political parties
2. Special committees
....

Economic/business organizations

1. Corporations
2. Chambers of commerce
3. Trade unions
....

Social/ civil society organizations

1. Religious organizations
2. Universities
3. NGO's
4. Think tanks
5. Bridge clubs
....

Outcomes/characteristics of the game:

| Greater Rule of Law | Higher Economic Growth | Better Business Environment | Higher Literacy Rates | Better Health for All |

[a] In this discussion, the "state" is distinct from the "government," which is a group of individuals heading some of the organizations of the state.

An organization that wants to improve law-and-order outcomes has a number of mechanisms at its disposal to manipulate incentives and elicit the desired behavior. For example, a Ministry of Interior could increase the salaries of its police officers. This could create individual incentives that may result in the recruitment of better qualified and more professional candidates to the police force. Increased competition for promotions as a result of the hiring of new recruits might provide current police officers with incentives to perform better, and the overall law enforcement outcomes in the country could improve.

However, decisions to alter organizational incentives are often intrinsically political because they entail zero-sum games. For example, in many contexts, law and order depends on the organizational or individual incentives of police officers to perform their duties effectively. If their salaries are too low or are not paid regularly, rule-of-law outcomes may suffer. To alter these incentives and increase police salaries, a Ministry of Interior must either raise more revenue or divert funds from other government programs toward this purpose. Other bureaucratic units or politicians would then be likely to oppose this change. Any change results in winners and losers, and because this is the case, individuals and organizations attempt to modify institutions in their favor: change "comes from the perceptions of the entrepreneurs in political and economic organizations that they could do better by altering the existing institutional framework at some margin" (North 1990, 8).

More importantly, bureaucratic organizations are not isolated entities. They follow "the rules of the game" (figure B1.1.1) and are subject to broader power relations in society. Even if our police officers were to receive better pay, the location of the Ministry of Interior within the broader institutional landscape would still matter much more than individual policemen's incentives for the purposes of final rule-of-law outcomes. If an official in the Ministry of the Interior were to receive direct orders from a discretionary executive to investigate only the alleged crimes of its political opponents and ignore those of its supporters, individual incentives would be simply supplanted by broader organizational incentives, turning rule-of-law outcomes into rule by law.

The following quote presents some findings from a recent survey related to procedural fairness and access to justice, and illustrates the primacy of political institutions over organizations—the traditional policy focus:

> Most people saw the problems with the police as being rooted not in law enforcement [organizations] … but in the political structure.… More than half of the members of the legal profession and the judiciary surveyed claimed that political connections played a role in access to justice and a fair trial. (Kleinfeld 2012, 90)

Until recently, the attention of policy makers working on the rule of law focused mostly on organizations (in blue squares in figure B1.1.1) and their incentives. The dominant assumption was that courts, police units, Ministries of Interior, and associations of lawyers in developing countries lacked resources and capacity to enforce, which led to implementation gaps between laws and practice. Throughout this book, we argue that the attention should instead turn from *organizations* to *institutions* (in green ovals in figure B1.1.1) and their equilibria. In particular, as in the police force example, we posit that *political institutions are the main factors that shape rule-of-law outcomes.*

Institutional Change and Accountability

The concept of "equilibrium" refers to the stability of institutions. The rules of the game reach "equilibrium" or steady state when all actors involved are better off accepting the situation rather than challenging it, and changes in the behavior of any stakeholder make everybody else adjust their own actions accordingly. Institutional equilibria can be either good or bad for rule-of-law outcomes. A suboptimal equilibrium would lock in incentives for discrimination of certain groups, corruption, and selective enforcement of laws and regulations. The policy goal should be the realignment of actors' behavior to reach a new equilibrium that can lead to a better societal outcome.

Two groups have the power to change formal institutions, causing shifts in rule of law equilibria: (a) those responsible for writing, amending, and interpreting formal laws—the executive, the legislature, and the judiciary—and (b) those responsible for implementing laws, regulating certain industries or organizations, and setting standards—the bureaucracy. Institutional change itself, represented by the red arrows in figure B1.1.1, originates from one of three main sources. *First*, the executive or the legislature may create a formal law. A new law strengthening the independence of the judiciary, for example, may lead to better enforcement because it prevents political interference. It may also lead to more equitable application of the law across individuals and organizations provided these have roughly equal access to justice. *Second*, the bureaucracy could change an economic institution. For example, an environmental regulatory agency could add carbon dioxide emissions to the list of pollutants, resulting in certain obligations and perhaps penalties for industries that emit carbon dioxide. As always, some private firms may benefit from new regulations of this kind, while others may lose out.

Third, informal rules or norms can change as well. Social institutions change when individuals and organizations, in the course of playing the game, modify their behavior and beliefs based on their interactions with other players. Business owners might be reluctant to hire women or ethnic minorities out of a belief that they would be less capable or dependable employees. This bias could change—and discrimination in hiring would occur less frequently—if business owners interacted more regularly with both groups. Women and minorities could hasten this process by lobbying political leaders to enact formal rules, for example, laws that promoted affirmative action or penalized discrimination. If enacted, an affirmative action law would not directly change the social norms or customs. Still, by compelling employers to hire women and minorities in greater numbers, unfavorable attitudes toward these groups might change and ultimately lead to a shift in social and cultural norms.

Institutions influence incentives and behavior, and these in turn affect the intended outcomes, such as equal access to justice or services, equitable taxation, and an end to corruption. Changing institutions to bring about particular outcomes can be a powerful tool for governments and donors alike. However, because of the strength of informal norms and traditions, institutional change that consists merely in replicating the formal rules of one country in another, without real buy-in from domestic reformers, may not be sufficient to bring about the desired change in rule-of-law outcomes:

> Societies that adopt the formal rules of another society (such as Latin American countries' adoption of constitutions like that of the United States) will have very different performance characteristics than the original country because

both the informal norms and the enforcement characteristics will be different. (North 1990, 25)

This is especially true for many early attempts at rule-of-law reform, when the formal laws of countries with strong rule of law were transplanted to others to little or no effect, or even a detrimental one, because there was neither the will to enforce them nor the willingness to comply with them.

Competition and *accountability* are the two answers to the question of what makes organizations promote higher rule-of law equilibria. Robust competition among different parties leads to the bureaucracy being insulated from political pressure since no party wants to risk political retaliation in case its rivals win elections in the future (Geddes 1996; Grzymala-Busse 2006; Moe 1989). Accountability can be internal or external (World Bank 2004). *Internal or horizontal* accountability relates to the responsibilities that organizations within the state, such as the bureaucracy, the legislature, and the judiciary, have to each other. In the absence of effective internal checks and balances, such as strong judiciaries, civil service commissions, and independent Supreme Audit Institutions, politicians can deprive bureaucracies of administrative capacity and staff them with their supporters, following a logic of clientelism.

External or vertical accountability relates to the sets of responsibilities among political, economic, and social organizations, on the one hand, and the state, on the other. Figure 1.2 illustrates these relations with black arrows. More vibrant scrutiny of state actions by organizations outside the state—such as civil society, business associations, the media, or opposition political parties—decreases the political incentives for bureaucrats misapplying laws and regulations:

> If you aim to protect the rights of women, organize a women's movement. If you want to protect the civil rights of black Americans, organize a civil rights movement…. The degree of justice or injustice depends on who wields power and for what ends. (Holmes 2003, 51)

In particular contexts, internal accountability can result in good outcomes even in the absence of robust external accountability. In several MENA countries, internal checks and balances did lead to higher rule-of-law outcomes despite the dominance of autocratic executives. For example, in the Islamic Republic of Iran, a complex institutional structure surrounding the drafting and voting of the annual budget enables meaningful policy debates between the Guardian Council and the Iranian legislature. In the Arab Republic of Egypt, parts of the judiciary have acted as a balance to the executive power of the Mubarak regime. Chapter 5 will present detailed evidence on the role of the courts as appeal venues in cases of unfair treatment by the bureaucracy in Jordan.

Enforcement Mechanisms

The third component of institutions, *enforcement mechanisms*, is at the center of this volume, for two reasons. *First*, in a world where the international diffusion of "good" laws templates has led to the relative cross-national uniformity of

Figure 1.2 External and Internal Accountability

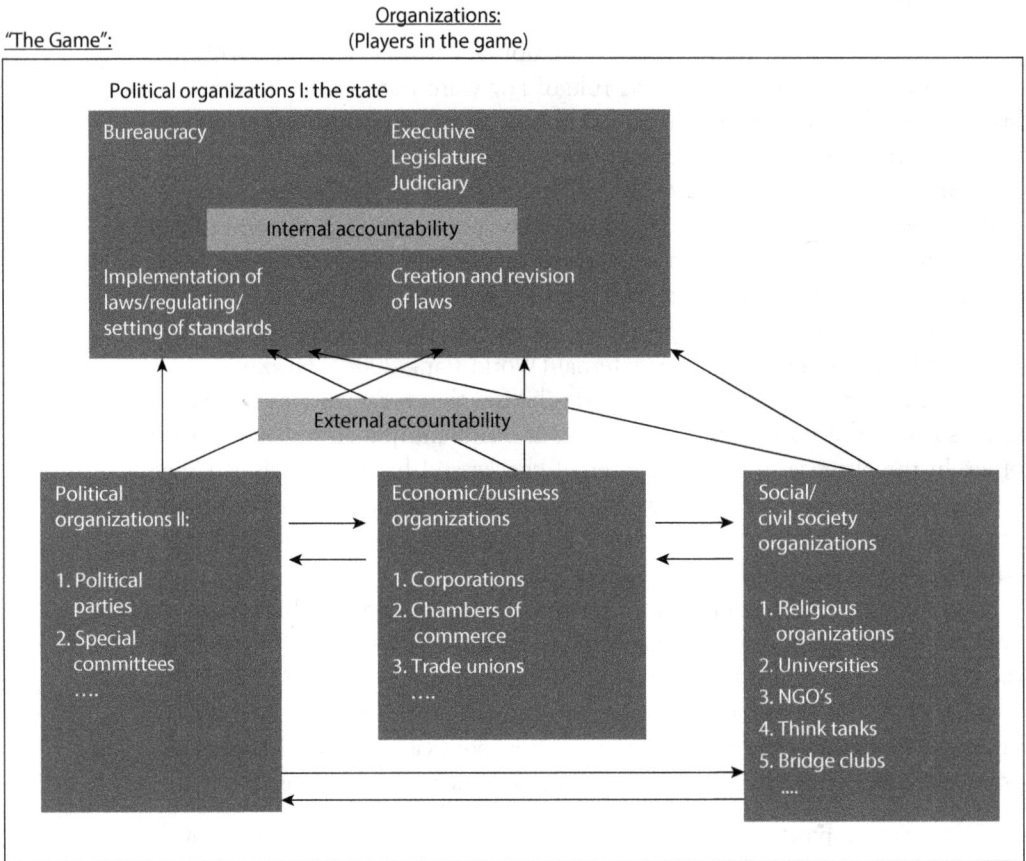

Figure layout labels:

"The Game":

Organizations:
(Players in the game)

Political organizations I: the state

Bureaucracy

Executive
Legislature
Judiciary

Internal accountability

Implementation of
laws/regulating/
setting of standards

Creation and revision
of laws

External accountability

Political
organizations II:

1. Political
   parties
2. Special
   committees
   ....

Economic/business
organizations

1. Corporations
2. Chambers of
   commerce
3. Trade unions
   ....

Social/
civil society
organizations

1. Religious
   organizations
2. Universities
3. NGO's
4. Think tanks
5. Bridge clubs
   ....

legal texts, and where social norms of political correctness preempt or forbid explicit discrimination, enforcement of laws and regulations on the ground remains the last bastion of unfair treatment. No formal law or informal norm exists that makes police officers exercise racial or ethnic profiling. Yet, abuse by police is widespread. *Second*, the actual enforcement of laws and regulations— such as tax collection, containing crime in the neighborhood, issuing business licenses and passports, or providing public health care—is the most concrete manifestation of the rule of law for ordinary citizens. These everyday encounters shape the public perceptions of procedural equity and fairness of treatment even more than litigation in courts.

To be sure, just like democracy, rule of law is an ideal rather than a reflection of reality. Discrimination and selective bureaucratic enforcement are persistent, even in the advanced industrial democracies of North America or Western Europe. Even there, powerful lobbies commonly lead to formal laws that increase inequalities between the few and the many. Tax offices often go after political opponents. Police officers at times abuse their mandate and discriminate on racial or ethnic grounds. Informal norms alive in bureaucracies sometimes lead to collusive policies that again privilege a minority over a majority. Courts and individual judges occasionally pass verdicts that are publicly perceived as blatantly unfair because of the political or economic influence of the parties to litigation. What makes rule-of-law problems serious is a question of magnitude, not of the existence of discriminatory practices. By contrast, in some other countries, the accountability channels described above are either completely missing or are so severely undermined by politics that they are used more to persecute than protect.

Documenting the systematic as opposed to random nature of unequal treatment or lack of fairness in the application of the law is a tall order. As indicated above, administrative lapses or imperfect laws and regulations, if severe, lead to an unpredictable legal environment that may result in inconsistent enforcement across individuals. Systematic (mis)application, on the other hand, suggests the intentional or deliberate decision to do so, but it is much harder to prove persuasively. Especially in autocratic countries where access to information is limited and the data opaque, the burden of proof can be costly. Moreover, systematic and random applications of the law sometimes blend together. Legal uncertainty, as an inferior rule-of-law outcome, can be the result of both administrative errors and intention.

In this book, we first try to distinguish the two categories, *random versus systematic enforcement* (or lack thereof), and bring political incentives into the picture to understand the latter. Whereas many studies assume that powerless or silent majorities, such as the poor and ethnic or racial minorities, are always disadvantaged by the systematic misapplication of the law, we try to understand all the possible configurations of imbalances in enforcement. In many cases, especially in autocratic contexts, powerful elites are more vulnerable to persecution through the law, or rule by law, than apolitical, silent majorities. For instance, "random" tax or work safety inspections are many times not so random because they aim at punishing politically assertive businesses. In the scholarship on the MENA region in particular, the thesis of "the vulnerability of the powerful" rests on solid ground.

Second, guided by the understanding of equilibria described in this chapter, we attempt to go beyond diagnosing enforcement problems to understand why they occur and persist. The general hypothesis is that *incentives generated by political institutions lead to variation in the implementation of laws and regulations.* If systematic enforcement is aligned with political incentives, then policies are more likely to be implemented. Conversely, laws will be selectively enforced only when desired outcomes run counter to the political interests of key stakeholders (figure B1.1.1) in the absence of internal or external accountability (figure 1.2).

In this regard, two features distinguish the MENA region from other parts of the world: (a) the lack of vigorous political competition and (b) the dominant role of the executive in policy making. These two characteristics have turned most MENA bureaucratic units into either underperforming hosts of public sector employees or compliant agents in a principal-agent relationship where the political principal is dominant. In light of such low expectations of effective implementation, the more interesting questions for future research become whether any "pockets of efficiency" exist within MENA bureaucracies; if so, why they have emerged, and, more generally, under what circumstances governments of the MENA region invest in bureaucratic performance and enforcement.

Policy Implications

Long-standing interest among donors in "capacity-building" has led to treatment of capacity, both explicitly and implicitly, as the key constraint to enforcement. Accordingly, building the capacity of a country's key organizations or subnational units should then lead to successful implementation. Unfortunately, different capacity building strategies over several decades have borne little fruit, and rethinking the merits of this approach is overdue. For many political economists and country experts, the failure of capacity-building efforts that do not take politics into account is not a surprise. Many of them have called on practitioners to look beyond capacity constraints and pay particular attention to political institutions and the incentives they generate. For this reason, we theorize bureaucratic capacity alongside political incentives, allowing for the existence of exogenous capacity constraints, and put forward an analytical matrix intended to help policy makers decide when and under what conditions interventions are likely to pay off or not. We propose to map select laws, regulations, or agencies to a matrix based on political economic incentives operating under capacity constraints (figure 1.3).

Quadrant 1 of figure 1.3 captures an ideal outcome in terms of enacting and enforcing laws. The bureaucratic agency performs well, has adequate resources, capacities are built in, and no political incentives exist to obstruct equitable treatment and fair enforcement. However, we explicitly avoid assessing the ultimate indicator of legal effectiveness, which is compliance with the law. In many cases, even if the state has the capacity and the will to enforce, general *compliance* will still be low in the absence of public trust in state institutions, government legitimacy, and perceptions of procedural fairness (Levi 1988; Brathwaite and Levi 2003).

In contrast, quadrant 4 of figure 1.3 describes the inferior equilibrium of low capacity and distorted (or lacking) political economic incentives to pass or enforce a law. Quadrant 2 describes rules and agencies that lack basic exogenous capacity but benefit from government willingness to pass and enforce laws and

Figure 1.3 Political Will and Capacity Matrix

Incentives/willingness to enforce	Capacity	
	High	Low
High	1	2
Low	3	4

regulations. Finally, quadrant 3 identifies those policies and agencies where a lack of political incentives to pass and enforce regulations exists even in the presence of adequate exogenous capacities.

Through the case study method, development practitioners could identify which policies and agencies fall within each quadrant, and derive conclusions that can be used to address similar problems relating to the rule of law in other countries in MENA and beyond. If a political economic analysis such as this one would point to the unlikelihood that a proposed reform will lead to a substantial improvement in the rule of law, then donors and development practitioners would be advised to direct their efforts toward policy areas where the incentives to implement and enforce are strongest.[3] If a technical assistance reform program still proceeds despite a lack of clear political incentives for implementation, the analysis can at the least help calibrate expectations with regard to outcomes. In such cases, it may still be worthwhile to help bureaucracies build administrative capacity in preparation for more ambitious reforms in the future.

To better understand how political incentives and capacity constraints lead to variation in the enforcement of laws and regulations in the MENA region, the next chapter spells out a series of hypotheses derived from the theoretical framework laid out in this chapter and tests them empirically using several cross-national rule-of-law datasets.

Notes

1. Appealing bureaucratic inequities can also impose high burdens on the judiciary. Just imagine the number of judges and courts necessary to challenge every corrupt or inequitable behavior of state bureaucrats.

2. However, organizations are not monolithic actors; their members may act independently of the broader collective.

3. For example, rule of law specialists in the United States Agency for International Development were of the opinion that this "will to reform" was so important that there was no point at all in pushing for reform if there was none (Kleinfeld 2012, 94).

References

Abrams, David, Marianne Bertrand, and Sendhil Mullainathan. 2007. "Do Judges Vary in Their Treatment of Race?" Research Paper P 11-07, University of Pennsylvania Law School, Philadelphia.

Berge, Lars Ivar Oppedal, Kjetil Bjorvatn, Simon Galle, Edward Miguel, Daniel Posner, Bertil Tungodden, and Kelly Zhang. 2015. "How Strong Are Ethnic Preferences?" NBER Working Paper 21715, National Bureau of Economic Research, Cambridge, Massachusetts.

Brathwaite, Valerie, and Margaret Levi. 2003. *Trust and Governance*. New York: Russell Sage Foundation.

Duflo, Esther, Greg Fischer, and Raghabendra Chattopadhyay. 2005. "Efficiency and Rent Seeking in Local Government in India." Working Paper, Massachusetts Institute of Technology, Cambridge, Massachusetts.

Geddes, Barbara. 1996. *Politician's Dilemma. Building State Capacity in Latin America.* Berkeley: University of California Press.

Grzymala-Busse, Anna. 2006. "The Discreet Charm of Formal Institutions: Postcommunist Party Competition and State Oversight." *Comparative Political Studies* 39 (10): 1–30.

Holmes, Stephen. 2003. "Lineages of the Rule of Law." In *Democracy and the Rule of Law,* edited by Jose Maria Maravall and Adam Przeworski, 19–61. Cambridge, UK: Cambridge University Press.

Kleinfeld, Rachel. 2012. *Advancing Rule of Law Reform Abroad: Next Generation Reform.* Washington, DC: Carnegie Endowment for International Peace.

Levi, Margaret. 1988. *Of Rule and Revenue.* Berkeley: University of California Press.

Moe, Terry M. 1989. "The Politics of Bureaucratic Structure." In *Can the Government Govern?,* edited by John E. Chubb and Paul E. Peterson, 267–329. Washington, DC: Brookings Institution Press.

North, Douglass. 1990. *Institutions, Institutional Change and Economic Performance.* Cambridge, MA: Cambridge University Press.

World Bank. 2004. *World Development Report 2004: Making Services Work for Poor People.* Washington, DC: World Bank.

CHAPTER 2

The Rule of Law in MENA: Hypotheses and Empirics

Introduction

Political institutions are fundamental to how power is allocated in society, because they affect bureaucratic organizations and their role as primary sites of enforcement of laws.[1] With specific reference to the Middle East and North Africa (MENA) region, this chapter formulates four hypotheses about how political institutions shape the enforcement of laws.

Hypotheses 1 and 2 theorize the relationships between political leaders and bureaucratic agencies in the region. Hypotheses 3 and 4 go one step farther and make the connection between social organizations and political leaders. They suggest that politicians respond (or not) to pressure from lobbies, vocal minority groups, or protest movements, and adjust enforcement accordingly. The chapter also empirically tests the four hypotheses, and examines the effect on enforcement of (a) political institutions, (b) bureaucratic capacity, as approximated by income, (c) political mobilization, and (d) ethnic and regional differences.

The data in the chapter come from two sources: the Global Integrity Index and the World Justice Project (WJP) datasets. Global Integrity provides scores on legal frameworks and the actual implementation of laws for the countries it measures. WJP, the most comprehensive and up-to-date dataset of its kind, measures how laws "are actually implemented in practice and experienced by those who are subject to them" (World Justice Project 2011). The WJP scoring ranks countries according to nine distinct factors and then calculates a general rule-of-law score for each country. Table 2.1 describes these nine factors.

As a prelude to the empirical analysis, we examine the implementation gap scores for the MENA region, and test whether the MENA region is different from the rest of the developing world in this regard. To do so, we subtract the *in reality* Global Integrity score ("Actual Implementation" score) from the *by law* score ("Legal Framework" score) to generate a measure of the implementation gap. Figure 2.1 plots these scores and the resulting implementation gap for several MENA countries. Table 2.2 presents a breakdown of average gap measures

Table 2.1 WJP Rule-of-Law Index—Nine Factors

Factor	Description
1. Constraints on government powers	Measures the extent to which those who govern are subject to law and accountable to citizens, as well as the degree to which their powers are limited.
2. Absence of corruption	In all three branches of government, this measures three forms of corruption: (a) bribery, (b) improper influence by public or private interests, and (c) misappropriation of public funds or other resources.
3. Order and security	Measures how well a society guarantees the security of persons and property in three regards: (a) absence of crime; (b) absence of civil conflict, including terrorism and armed conflict; and (c) absence of violence as a socially acceptable means to redress personal grievances.
4. Fundamental rights	Measures the protection of basic human rights. That is, the effective protection of freedom of expression, religion, privacy, assembly, basic labor rights, due process under law, and so on.
5. Open government	Measures the extent to which (a) written laws are clear and made public; (b) the public is able to take part in the formulation and administration of laws (through, for example, petitions and public consultations).
6. Regulatory enforcement	Measures the fair and effective enforcement of administrative regulations. This includes (a) the absence of improper influence by public officials or private interests; (b) adherence to administrative procedures that are fair, consistent, and predictable; and (c) the assurance that the government cannot confiscate private property without adequate compensation.
7. Civil justice	Measures accessibility to civil justice in relation to affordability, effectiveness, impartiality, and cultural competence.
8. Criminal justice	Measures the effectiveness of criminal justice, including investigative capacity, impartiality, and the protection of the rights of the accused.
9. Informal justice	Measures the effectiveness of "informal" systems of law, including traditional, ethnic groupings, and religious courts, in resolving disputes.
	These systems often play a large role in societies, where formal legal institutions fail to provide effective remedies for large segments of the population.

Source: World Justice Project 2011.

Figure 2.1 Global Integrity Scores in the MENA Region

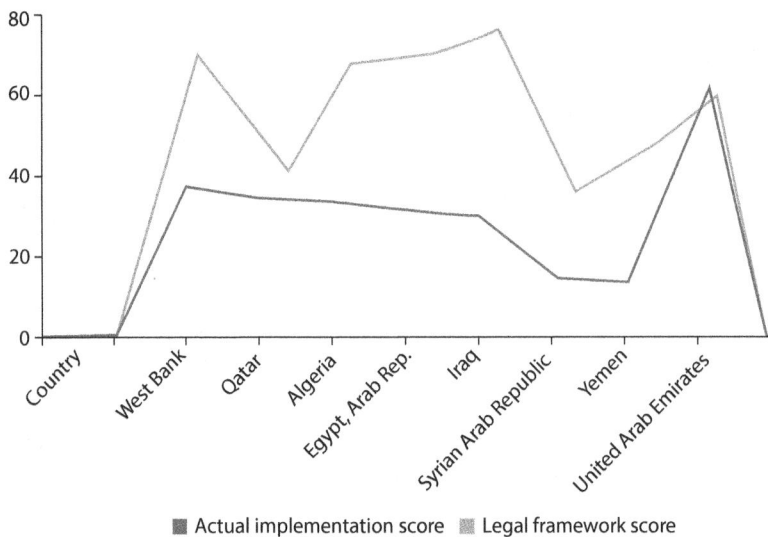

■ Actual implementation score   ▨ Legal framework score

Source: Global Integrity Report (various years).
Note: Scores range from 0 to 100.

Table 2.2 Global Integrity—Implementation Gap Measures by Region and Income Group

Region	Income				
	Low	Lower middle	Upper middle	High	Total
Middle East and North Africa	...	**28.9**	**25.6**	**3.3**	**22.0**
		6	**4**	**3**	**13**
Eastern Europe and Central Asia	36.1	32.0	32.4	18.9	30.7
	2	5	11	3	21
East Asia and Pacific	27.7	34.2	25.2	...	30.7
	1	4	2		7
Latin America and the Caribbean	...	38.7	30.2	...	32.7
		3	7		10
Sub-Saharan Africa	31.8	27.7	30.8	...	30.8
	10	3	2		15
South Asia	30.7	38.4	...	...	34.5
	2	2			4
Developed Countries	...	...	...	13.3	13.3
				6	6
Total	31.9	32.4	30.1	12.2	28.3
	15	23	26	12	76

Source: Global Integrity Report (various years).
Note: Implementation Gap = Actual Implementation score – Legal Framework score;
... = no observations for that category.

by region and country-income categories, following the classification system of the World Bank.[2]

Results in table 2.2 do not confirm a frequently made claim that MENA suffers from a wider implementation gap than other regions. If anything, MENA has the lowest gap levels among developing regions—although the general average for MENA is strongly affected by the low gaps in the three high-income Gulf Cooperation Council countries with the Global Integrity data (Kuwait, Qatar, and the United Arab Emirates). Looking more closely at the lower-middle-income and upper-middle-income groups, MENA performs slightly better than the average, and essentially fares no better or worse than the other developing regions.

Hypothesis 1: Political Institutions

The character of political institutions is one of the main reasons policies are implemented selectively rather than comprehensively. Most MENA countries range between autocracy and hybrid polities that combine some democratic features, such as limited multiparty competition with autocratic restraints on political rights and civil liberties. In both contexts, the rule *of* law tends to be supplanted by regimes that rule *by* law, where the top echelons of the state are not subject to rules and regulations, procedural fairness, and equitable treatment. This makes rule-of-law problems severe and long-lasting, since the accountability relations depicted in figure 1.2 of chapter 1 are either weak or missing.

Nonetheless, this does not mean that *all* laws and regulations will be selectively enforced. Decision makers will bolster those organizations that serve their interests to maintain their institutional equilibrium of choice and deprive others that can undermine their authority over resources. Political incumbents often need to offer key elites some reward if they are to remain in office. Regulatory enforcement of policies and laws that generate rents to core political supporters or prevent opponents from posing a credible threat is therefore more systematic (Ames 1987; Bueno de Mesquita et al. 2003; Geddes 1994).

If leaders oppose a particular institution of the rule of law, they will do everything in their power to block its implementation. The most effective way is to undermine the organizations tasked with enforcing the law; a law on the statute books becomes stillborn when implementing agencies are denied the funding, human resources, or political support to enforce it. Conversely, organizations such as government ministries and agencies that serve the interests of decision makers will receive all the resources they need. Accordingly, in countries ruled by authoritarian regimes, funds can be chronically short for the most basic services and infrastructure, such as a well-equipped health clinic or a paved road, while there would appear to be no lack of funds for the military and the security services.

Political interests can be expected to deliberately reduce law enforcement across some geographic areas. Organizations in districts more important to a regime's political survival will be better supplied, staffed, funded, and politically supported. Intergovernmental revenue transfers and poverty maps that guide the targeting of social spending programs to different locations often reflect political incentives to stifle opposition or, in the context of the MENA region, to prevent the opposition from mobilizing.

Hybrid political institutions complicate the law even more. While noncompetitive autocracies use openly coercive tactics to quell political dissent and silence critics, competitive authoritarian states are more concerned with their international standing and legitimacy. They are more likely to accommodate social concerns. They therefore resort to "legal repression" and implement "good" laws selectively and arbitrarily to punish political opponents. In this way, laws relating to taxation, corruption, and libel and defamation become "a shield for friends of the regime and a weapon against its enemies," increasing the cost to the opposition of taking collective action (Durand 2003, 463; Levitsky and Way 2010).

Regulatory uncertainty is a key tool for controlling society, and this is characteristic of many institutions in the MENA region. Under the Ben Ali regime in Tunisia, for example, the failure to reimburse substantial bank loans or the failure to comply with tax legislation were penalized or tolerated depending on a business owner's relations with officials of the Democratic Constitutional Rally party (Hibou 2006). The in-depth case studies of Morocco, Tunisia, and Jordan in this book also discuss regime transitions as shifts in accountability relations, and tease out their effects on the rule of law.

We next turn to a regression analysis of the effect of political institutions on the implementation gap as measured in table 2.2. We use three variables as proxies for political institutions. The first, a measure of political accountability, is known as the W-score. This is a five-point measure that runs from 0 (low accountability) to 1 (high accountability). It is based on the Selectorate Theory described in box 2.1 (Bueno de Mesquita et al. 2003).

The second variable is a binary measure of democracy. It comes from the Democracy and Dictatorship (D-and-D) Revisited dataset (Cheibub, Gandhi, and Vreeland 2010), which extends an earlier dataset developed by Przeworski et al. 2000. The data are from 2008.

The third variable is also a binary measure of democracy constructed from the well-known polity2 variable from the Polity IV dataset (Marshall, Jaggers, and Gurr 2011).

A country is coded as a democracy if it had a polity2 score of six or greater in 2009 (or 2010 if data were unavailable in 2009). A country is coded as a hybrid

---

Box 2.1 The Selectorate Theory

Chapter 1 showed how political competition can have beneficial effects on rule-of-law outcomes. Besides competition, the *size* of the group of individuals constitutionally designated to select political leaders also matters. According to the Selectorate Theory of Bueno de Mesquita et al. (2003), political institutions determine the size of the group of citizens whose support political leaders need to retain power (that is the proportion of the population to whom leaders are ultimately accountable). This is referred to as the size of the leader's winning coalition, W.

Political leaders maintain the support of their winning coalition by providing private goods to their supporters (jobs, government contracts, and the like) and by providing public goods such as policies that stimulate economic growth or promote development. When the political institutions are such that W is small, a political leader is accountable only to some individuals. In this case, it is more efficient to provide private goods directly to that small group of individuals. By contrast, when political institutions are such that W is large, a political leader must keep many individuals happy. In this case, providing private benefits to such a large group is almost impossible.

Moreover, in light of finite resources, as W increases, the value of the private goods that each supporter receives decreases. After a certain level of W, it is no longer efficient to focus on providing private goods to one's supporters. Instead, it becomes more efficient to focus one's limited resources on the provision of public goods, which can reach and benefit many individuals simultaneously. In other words, *the incentives to pass and enforce laws benefiting the public increase as the size of the winning coalition increases; that is, when political leaders are accountable to a larger proportion of the population.*

To test the Selectorate Theory, we developed a rough measure of accountability, the W-score, which combines the degree of political competition and the size of the winning coalition.

Rules on Paper, Rules in Practice • http://dx.doi.org/10.1596/978-1-4648-0886-9

regime if its polity2 score is between minus five and five, and as an autocracy if its polity2 score is below minus 5. We obtained both democracy variables from the Quality of Government composite dataset of the World Bank's World Development Indicators online database.[3]

Table 2.3 presents the results of the regression analysis. In column 1 we present the regional means recalculated from table 2.2, with DEV as the excluded region. The implementation gap is greater for every developing region when compared to DEV. These estimates are also statistically significant, except for MNA, for which the regional average implementation gap is lower, as shown above.

Interestingly, the accountability W-score measure (column 2) and the Cheibub, Gandhi, and Vreeland. (2010) democracy measure (column 3) are not

Table 2.3 Political Institutions and Implementation Gap Regression Analysis

	1	2	3	4	5
Middle East and North Africa	8.7	−6.9	−5.2	−5.5	−2.5
	(5.6)	(7.6)	(7.0)	(6.1)	(6.0)
Eastern Europe and Central Asia	17.4	6.8	7.0	5.8	8.3
	(5.2)***	(6.2)	(6.1)	(5.5)	(5.5)
East Asia and Pacific	17.4	1.0	−0.1	1.4	5.9
	(6.3)***	(7.6)	(7.5)	(6.7)	(6.8)
Latin America and the Caribbean	19.4	8.2	9.4	9.2	10.8
	(5.8)***	(6.5)	(6.3)	(5.8)	(5.7)*
Sub-Saharan Africa	17.5	−3.0	−4.5	−3.5	−1.0
	(5.4)***	(7.9)	(8.0)	(7.1)	(7.0)
South Asia	21.2	0.8	−0.2	−0.4	2.5
	(7.3)***	(9.0)	(9.0)	(8.3)	(8.1)
Log (GNI pc)		−4.3	−4.8	−4.3	−3.3
		(1.4)***	(1.4)***	(1.3)***	(1.4)**
Log (population)		0.7	0.8	0.8	0.7
		(1.0)	(1.1)	(1.0)	(1.0)
W-score		−9.7			
		(7.6)			
Democracy (D and D)			−5.0		
			(3.3)		
Democracy (Polity IV)				−7.0	−0.6
				(2.7)**	(3.9)
Hybrid regimes (Polity IV)					9.2
					(4.1)**
Constant	13.3	55.3	56.1	51.8	36.6
	(4.6)***	(24.1)**	(24.2)**	(21.9)**	(22.3)
R^2	0.22	0.38	0.37	0.43	0.47
N	76	73	74	73	73

Note: Standard errors in parentheses. Coefficient estimates significantly different from zero at 90 percent (*), 95 percent (**), 99 percent (***) confidence.

statistically significant, although their sizes are somewhat large and in the correct downward direction. The polity-based measures, by contrast, are significant—suggesting that the effect of institutions may be nonlinear and require a higher degree of disaggregation than that measured with the Cheibub, Gandhi, and Vreeland (2010) variable. More precisely, column 4 shows that having a democratic political regime (polity2 score > 5) is associated with a lower implementation gap, of 7 percentage points.

Column 5 shows the effects of hybrid regimes. Hybrid regimes are not complete dictatorships, but not full democracies either. Outwardly, they attempt to mimic the democratic regimes (with occasional elections) but the daily state-citizen relations are more similar to autocracies. Competitive authoritarianism is a well-known type of hybrid regime. Following standard practice, we construct a dummy variable for a hybrid regime based on the Polity IV polity2 variable. A country is considered to have a hybrid regime if the polity2 variable is greater than or equal to −5 and less than or equal to 5 (−5 <= polity2 <= 5). Column 5 indicates that the democratic political regime variable loses significance when we also include a dummy variable for hybrid regimes, and the hybrid regime variable is significant at the 99 percent level of statistical confidence.[4] This tells us that hybrid regimes are highly correlated with implementation gaps, and that the effect we see in column 4 is the effect of hybrid regimes working through the democratic regimes variable.[5] A hybrid regime increases the implementation gap on average by 9.2 percentage points. In addition, including the polity2 democratic and hybrid regime dummies decreased the effect of the income variable by over 1.5 percentage points, and decreases its statistical significance—a further testament to the influence of hybrid regimes.

When we add log income and population to the regressions in columns 2 to 5, we note that income is significant but population is not. Moreover, the negative coefficient estimate on log income signifies that the implementation gap decreases as income increases. Of further interest is the effect of inclusion of the income variable on the regional dummies. We also see no difference among developing regions, including between MENA and other regions—as we noticed in the lower-middle-income and upper-middle-income columns in table 2.2.

Hence, we find that, first, higher income, which could signify higher bureaucratic capacity, leads to smaller implementation gaps. Second, hybrid regimes lead to larger implementation gaps.

Table 2.4 breaks down countries included in the regression analysis of table 2.2, column 5, by regime type and region. We see that in 2009 MENA accounted for the second-highest number of hybrid regimes, after Sub-Saharan Africa (SSA), with six countries falling in this category. Table 2.5 lists all the countries in MENA by regime type, regardless of whether they were included in the regression analysis. As noted in chapter 1, autocracies and hybrid regimes are especially prevalent in the region.[6]

Table 2.4 Regime Type by Region as Included in the Regression in Table 2.3, Column 5

Region	Regime			
	Autocracy	Hybrid	Democracy	Total
Middle East and North Africa	5	6	1	12
Eastern Europe and Central Asia	3	4	13	20
East Asia and Pacific	2	1	4	7
Latin America and the Caribbean	0	2	8	10
Sub-Saharan Africa	0	8	6	14
South Asia	0	2	2	4
Developed Countries	0	0	6	6
Total	10	23	40	73

Source: Polity IV database.

Table 2.5 MENA Regime Types Based on the Polity IV Polity2 Measure—2009 Data

Autocracy	Hybrid	Democracy
Morocco	Algeria	Lebanon
Libya	Tunisia	
Syrian Arab Republic	Egypt, Arab Rep.	
Iran, Islamic Rep.	Jordan	
Saudi Arabia	Iraq	
Kuwait	Yemen, Rep.	
Bahrain	Djibouti	
Qatar		
United Arab Emirates		
Oman		

Source: Polity IV database and authors' asessments.

Hypothesis 2: Bureaucratic Capacity and Income

The theoretical emphasis on political institutions notwithstanding, we recognize that the incentives that shape the rule of law often evolve within exogenous capacity constraints. In low-income countries, inadequate administrative and fiscal capacity presents major challenges to implementation. These constraints need to be taken into account when assessing the effect of incentives on outcomes. Exogenous extractive capacity is particularly important with regard to the implementation of tax policy.

If the tax authority has limited capacity to collect taxes and if it anticipates low compliance among certain categories of taxpayers, it is not likely to invest resources in chasing payment, opting for a pragmatic approach. We will see in chapter 3 that weak tax administrations are less likely to audit small and medium enterprises or collect taxes in areas notorious for their failure to pay tax.

The capacity of the state to enforce tax laws also shapes the preferences and demands of social, economic, and political groups. In many developing countries, including in MENA, whenever public sector employees believed their government lacked sufficient capacity to enforce social insurance legislation on pensions, disability, and unemployment insurance, they were more likely to demand private schemes rather than universal public coverage. Such preferences, shaped by uncertainty about the future stream of redeemable benefits if the government could not collect contributions effectively, ultimately led to different formal laws and regulations (Mares and Carnes 2009).

For regression analyses, we use gross national income (GNI) per capita as a proxy for administrative capacity to examine its effect on rule-of-law outcomes. The assumption is that countries in the low-income group often lack the necessary resources to build well-functioning bureaucracies. While imperfect, it is the only consistent cross-national measure without major data gaps that allows the examination of empirical patterns.[7] We use two dependent variables. The first is the composite WJP rule-of-law index, and the second is WJP's factor 6, *regulatory enforcement*—the aspect of the rule of law that is the primary focus of this volume. Both variables range from 0 to 100, with 0 representing the lowest rule-of-law outcomes and 100 the highest.

In 2012, WJP ranked rule-of-law outcomes in 97 countries, based on data from surveys in 2009, 2011, and 2012. Table 2.6 shows averages for the general rule-of-law index by seven regions and four income classes, following the classification system of the World Bank. Similar tables for eight of the nine WJP

Table 2.6 Income and WJP's General Rule-of-Law Index

Region	Income				
	Low	Lower middle	Upper middle	High	Total
Middle East and North Africa	...	50.0	53.3	64.0	53.9
		2	4	1	7
Eastern Europe and Central Asia	45.0	49.4	53.0	67.3	55.9
	1	5	9	6	21
East Asia and Pacific	41.0	50.5	53.7	73.0	53.0
	1	4	3	1	9
Latin America and the Caribbean	...	44.8	52.5	...	50.6
		4	12		16
Sub-Saharan Africa	45.5	46.5	63.0	...	47.8
	10	6	2		18
South Asia	45.0	46.0	...	...	45.6
	2	3			5
Developed Countries	...	...	...	78.4	78.4
				21	21
Total	45.1	47.7	53.6	75.4	57.4
	14	24	30	29	97

Source: World Justice Project dataset (2009, 2011, and 2012).
Note: ... = no observations for that category.

Rules on Paper, Rules in Practice • http://dx.doi.org/10.1596/978-1-4648-0886-9

rule-of-law factors are included in Appendix A. With each box in the table, we present the average rule-of-law index for the countries in each region and income category pair, as well as the number of countries included in the pairing.

A total of 14 countries were categorized as low income, 24 as lower-middle income, 30 as upper-middle income, and 29 as high income. The total scores in the last row of the table indicate that a strong correlation between income and the general rule-of-law index. As income increases, the rule-of-law index also increases, from an average of 45.1 for low income, to 47.7 for lower-middle income, to 53.6 for upper-middle income, and to 75.4 for high-income countries. These numbers already confirm the bureaucratic capacity hypothesis.

That said, income as a proxy for administrative capacity is not the sole determinant of rule-of-law outcomes. Notice in particular the large increase of 21 percentage points when we move from the upper-middle income group to the high-income group. This is mostly a function of the 78.4 average rule-of-law score for developed countries, all of which are high income. Yet the high-income developing countries (such as the Gulf countries in MENA) do not score as high as the developed countries on rule-of-law outcomes, indicating—as we show below—that other factors are at play.

For a comparison between MENA and other regions, the rows in table 2.6 are arranged so that MENA is the top and the others follow. The regions are ranked in descending order according to the number of high-income countries they include. Accordingly, Eastern Europe and Central Asia (ECA), with six high-income countries, comes immediately after MENA, East Asia and Pacific (EAP)—with one high-income country—comes next, and so on. Developed countries come last. Given this ordering, it is not a surprise to see the general correlation between income and rule-of-law transfers to our rule-of-law results by region—with regions comprising more higher-income countries ranking higher on the general rule-of-law index. ECA has the highest score of all developing regions with 55.9, followed by MENA with 53.9, EAP with 53.0, and Latin America and the Caribbean (LAC) with 50.6. The two lower-income regions, SSA and South Asia (SAR), have the lowest scores, with 47.8 and 45.6, respectively. Finally, as mentioned above, developed countries of North America, Western Europe, and Asia (DEV) score the highest, at 78.4.

A few points about these regional averages should be noted because they are important for subsequent analysis. First, MENA as a whole performs better than other regions, with an average rule-of-law score similar to the higher-income ECA, EAP, and LAC regions. Second, all the high-income ECA countries are members of the European Union (EU), and two of the nine upper-middle income ECA countries (Bulgaria and Romania) are also members of the European Union. Hence, rule-of-law averages for these two ECA groups may be higher, given the requirements and demonstration effects of being members of the European Union.

Third, there is quite a lot of variability within regions by income categories. In MENA (with seven countries), the rule-of-law general score for the one high-income country, the United Arab Emirates (64.0), is much higher than the average of the upper-middle income countries, the Islamic Republic of Iran, Jordan, Lebanon, and Tunisia (53.3), and this score, in turn, is higher than the average for the lower-middle income countries, the Arab Republic of Egypt and Morocco (50.0). With the exception of LAC and SAR, this same variability exists within other regions.

Given this variability among income groups within regions, it is important when comparing MENA with other regions to also make this comparison by income group. Compared in this way, MENA performs reasonably well. In the lower-middle income group, the average for MENA countries (Egypt and Morocco) is 50.0, the highest score among regions (tied with EAP) and above the 47.7 average of all regions. In the upper-middle income group, the average for MENA countries (the Islamic Republic of Iran, Jordan, Lebanon, and Tunisia) is 53.3, which is around the same for the higher-income regions ECA, EAP, and LAC, but below the average for Botswana and South Africa in SSA. The United Arab Emirates, however, does not perform as well. At 64.0, it has the lowest score in the high-income category. Nevertheless, its comparators are the high-income ECA countries, all of which are in the EU, the Republic of Korea, and the entire DEV group.

With the exception of the high-income group of MENA countries (which are compared with developed countries), rule-of-law scores in MENA are slightly above average in lower-middle income countries and essentially on a par with the upper-middle income countries in other regions.

Next, we examine the effect of income as a proxy of bureaucratic capacity on WJP's factor 6, regulatory enforcement. As described in chapter 1, selective regulatory enforcement is a key tool used by governing elites to control society and to reward supporters and punish enemies. WJP ranks countries on this factor by "how well regulations are implemented and enforced" and goes on to say, "This includes the absence of improper influence by public officials or private interests; adherence to administrative procedures that are fair, consistent, and predictable; and freedom from government taking of private property without adequate compensation" (World Justice Project 2011, 13). As with the general rule-of-law index, we see that factor 6 is also highly correlated with income, with all regions showing the same trend of increasing scores as income rises (table 2.7). Therefore, we find support for the bureaucratic capacity hypothesis for the regulatory enforcement measure of rule of law as well.

A comparison of scores within income groups shows that MENA is not unlike other regions of the developing world. Differences in total regional scores would appear to be a function of the number of countries in each income group, with regions having a greater number of high-income countries scoring better. Moreover, for the high-income group, all high-income countries in MENA, ECA, and EAP have lower scores than the DEV region, and the averages are about the same, even for ECA countries that are members of the European Union. This suggests that some room for improvement exists for high-income countries in the developing regions. As before, MENA is no better or any worse than other regions.

Table 2.7 Income and WJP's Factor 6 (Regulatory Enforcement) Index

Region	Income				
	Lower	Lower middle	Upper middle	High	Total
Middle East and North Africa	...	44.5	51.5	65.0	51.4
		2	4	1	7
Eastern Europe and Central Asia	43.0	45.2	50.7	60.0	51.7
	1	5	9	6	21
East Asia and Pacific	33.0	47.0	48.0	67.0	48.0
	1	4	3	1	9
Latin America and the Caribbean	...	44.3	51.3	...	49.6
		4	12		16
Sub-Saharan Africa	39.5	44.8	62.5	...	43.8
	10	6	2		18
South Asia	40.0	43.0	...	...	41.8
	2	3			5
Developed Countries	...	...	...	75.9	75.9
				21	21
Total	39.4	44.9	51.6	71.9	54.2
	14	24	30	29	97

Source: World Justice Project dataset (2009, 2011, and 2012).
Note: ... = no observations for that category.

Although the factor 6 average for the MENA upper-middle income group was 51.5, this masked a great deal of variability. When considering subfactor 6.2 alone, Jordan scored a high of 67, while the Islamic Republic of Iran and Tunisia both scored 55, and Lebanon scored just 26. Moreover, to get a sense of the variability among countries within country-region groups, figure 2.2 lists the scores for several countries on one of the subfactors of factor 6: WJP Subfactor 6.2 (the question "Are government regulations applied and enforced without improper influence?").

Given this variability within groups, a more formal regression analysis was used to confirm the findings. Beginning with WJP's general rule-of-law index, the mean values given in table 2.2 are recalculated using regression analysis. These recalculated means are listed in column 1 of table 2.4. DEV is the excluded region. It is easy to confirm the results from the last column of table 2.2. The average for DEV is the constant in the regression, or 78.4. For MENA, the average for the general rule-of-law index is 78.4 − 24.5 = 53.9, as we see in table 2.2, and so on for the other regions. As expected, the regional dummies are all statistically significant from zero at the 99 percent confidence level.

In column 2, measures of log income (GNI per capita in current US dollars) and log population are added. These numbers are for 2009 and come from the World Development Indicators as compiled by the Quality of Government dataset (Teorell et al. 2013; World Bank 2013).[8] We use 2009 data instead of data for later years, because some of our WJP data come from a survey conducted in 2009. The rest of the data come from surveys conducted in 2011 and 2012.

Figure 2.2 WJP Subfactor 6.2

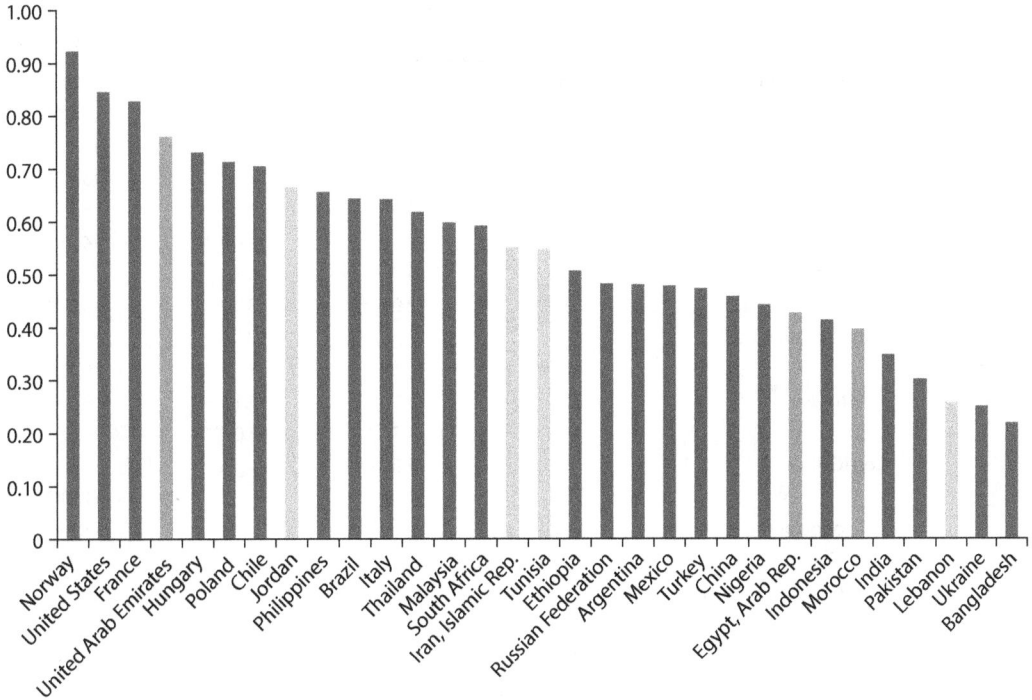

Source: World Justice Project dataset (2009, 2011, and 2012).

Both of these measures are significant at the 99 percent confidence level, with higher rule-of-law scores correlated with higher levels of income and lower levels of population. Substantively, we find that an increase of income by 2.7 times is associated with a general rule-of-law score increase of 6.8 points (table 2.8). For example, if we move from a country with a GNI per capita of about US$3,000 (roughly the GNI per capita of Morocco) to one with a GNI per capital of about US$8,000, the general rule-of-law score increases by 6.8 points.

We present similar regression results with factor 6 as the dependent variable in columns 3 and 4. Results are similar to those in columns 1 and 2, with increases in GNI per capita associated with higher factor 6 scores. The coefficient estimate on log income is even greater, at 7.4. Thus, an increase of income by 2.7 times is associated with a factor 6 score increase of 7.4 points. The results of the regression analysis shown in columns 2 and 4 therefore confirm that greater bureaucratic capacity is correlated with higher levels of rule-of-law outcomes.

Another important finding from columns 2 and 4 is that when we include income and population, the effects of the EAP, SSA, and SAR regional dummy variables become insignificant, with coefficients close to zero. For example, the indicator variable for SAR goes from −32.8 and statistically significant (column 1)

Table 2.8 Hypothesis 2—Bureaucratic Capacity

	General Rule-of-Law Index		Fac. 6—Enforcement	
	1	2	3	4
Middle East and North Africa	**−24.5**	**−11.1**	**−24.5**	**−9.9**
	(3.8)*	**(3.3)***	**(4.4)***	**(4.2)****
Eastern Europe and Central Asia	−22.5	−10.7	−24.2	−11.1
	(2.7)***	(2.7)***	(3.1)***	(3.4)***
East Asia and Pacific	−25.4	−4.7	−27.9	−6.2
	(3.4)***	(3.6)	(4.0)***	(4.5)
Latin America and the Caribbean	−27.8	−13.8	−26.3	−11.1
	(2.9)***	(2.9)***	(3.3)***	(3.6)***
Sub-Saharan Africa	−30.6	−3.5	−32.1	−2.7
	(2.8)***	(4.1)	(3.2)***	(5.1)
South Asia	−32.8	−3.1	−34.1	−3.0
	(4.3)***	(4.7)	(5.0)***	(6.0)
Log (GNI pc)		6.8		7.4
		(0.9)***		(1.1)***
Log (population)		−2.1		−1.7
		(0.5)***		(0.7)**
Constant	78.4	40.5	75.9	25.6
	(1.9)***	(12.9)***	(2.2)***	(16.2)
R^2	0.66	0.81	0.60	0.74
N	97	96	97	96

Note: Standard errors in parentheses. Coefficient estimates significantly different from zero at 90 percent (*), 95 percent (**), 99 percent (***) confidence.

to −3.1 but not statistically significant from zero—essentially zero (column 2). This indicates that the differences seen in these regions from the DEV group of developed countries can be explained by income and population.

This is not the case for MENA, ECA, and LAC. That is, when taking into account income and population, MENA, ECA, and LAC are still below the DEV region average. With a coefficient of −11.1 for the MENA dummy used in the general rule-of-law regression (column 2), and after controlling for population and income, MENA countries on average had a rule-of-law score 11.1 points below the average for developed countries. The effect was similar for ECA and somewhat stronger for LAC. Therefore, income and population do not explain all the variation in rule-of-law outcomes that we observe in MENA, ECA, and LAC.

Hypothesis 3: Mobilization and Collective Action

Policy outcomes often favor powerful social or economic groups able to mobilize and lobby effectively to the detriment of the interests of ordinary citizens. The power of collective action is also at work with regard to law enforcement. If elite groups are able to organize and resist regulatory implementation, governments may be unwilling to challenge them.

In Morocco, the ability of the textile and apparel industry to organize gave manufacturers important leverage in setting the pace of trade policy implementation (Cammett 2006). More recently, the Qatari government came under international scrutiny when human rights organizations reported that it consistently failed to enforce labor laws meant to protect migrant workers against frequent abuses by domestic employers under the *kefala* (employment sponsorship) system (Morin 2013; Moskowitz 2013).

Whereas Qatari employers have lobbied the government and obtained policy advantages, foreign workers have been unable to demand better enforcement of labor laws and regulations because they are not allowed to join labor unions, change employers, or leave the country without their employer's permission.

The WJP General Population Survey provides a means to measure political mobilization and collective action. It includes detailed survey data for 67 of the 97 countries covered by the WJP in 2012, including five MENA countries: Egypt, the Islamic Republic of Iran, Lebanon, Tunisia, and the United Arab Emirates. The survey polled about 1,000 respondents in each country and attempted to be representative of gender, income, and population among the three largest cities in a country. Among the questions asked in the survey was whether: "In practice, people in this neighborhood can get with others and present their concerns to members of Congress [or Parliament]" (Questions 37h). The variable assigned to responses ranges from 0 (strongly disagree with the question) to 1 (strongly agree). The average response to this question is used to measure political mobilization.

Results for the general rule-of-law index were not significant and are not shown. Results for the index of regulatory enforcement are shown in table 2.9. As before, the table includes log income, log population, and (in separate regressions) our four political institutions variables. To these, the measure of mobilization is added.

First, strong results are seen for the mobilization variable. The coefficient estimates for this variable are statistically significant from zero at the 95 percent confidence level for all four regressions, with an average coefficient estimate of about 34. This means that if we move from an average mobilization score of 0.48 (the 10th percentile in the sample) to 0.70 (the 90th percentile), the regulatory enforcement score increases by 7.5 points. This effect is somewhat stronger than a 2.7 times increase in GNI per capita and almost twice as large as moving from an autocracy to a democracy.

Another interesting finding is that, except for the ECA dummy variable in the column 3 regression, none of the regional dummy variables is significant. That is, for regulatory enforcement, when we control for population, income, and average mobilization, regional differences from the DEV group disappear.

Therefore, we find that our measure shows political mobilization has a substantively significant effect on regulatory enforcement outcomes, but no effect on the general rule-of-law index.

Chapter 3 also shows how business groups and associations have influenced tax policy enforcement in Morocco, bringing qualitative validation to this hypothesis.

Rules on Paper, Rules in Practice • http://dx.doi.org/10.1596/978-1-4648-0886-9

Table 2.9 Hypothesis 3—Political Mobilization & WJP Regulatory Enforcement

	1	2	3	4
Middle East and North Africa	−4.8	−6.3	−6.8	−6.9
	(6.1)	(5.6)	(5.4)	(5.9)
Eastern Europe and Central Asia	−6.9	−7.5	−8.2	−7.3
	(4.7)	(4.7)	(4.7)*	(4.8)
East Asia and Pacific	−0.5	−1.9	−3.0	−2.2
	(7.5)	(7.3)	(7.3)	(7.3)
Latin America and the Caribbean	−7.1	−7.0	−7.3	−6.8
	(4.6)	(4.7)	(4.6)	(4.7)
Sub-Saharan Africa	4.6	3.4	3.7	3.2
	(7.8)	(7.7)	(7.6)	(7.7)
South Asia	3.1	2.9	2.9	2.8
	(8.2)	(8.3)	(8.2)	(8.2)
log (GNI pc)	6.8	6.6	6.3	6.7
	(1.5)***	(1.6)***	(1.5)***	(1.5)***
log (population)	−1.8	−1.7	−1.8	−2.0
	(0.9)**	(0.9)*	(0.9)**	(0.8)**
democracy (D and D)	2.9			
	(3.1)			
democracy (Polity IV)		1.9		
		(2.8)		
hybrid reg. (Polity IV)			−4.0	
			(2.8)	
W-score				1.6
				(6.5)
Political mobilization	**33.1**	**34.3**	**35.5**	**32.0**
	(15.5)**	**(16.1)****	**(15.9)****	**(15.9)****
constant	6.8	7.8	12.1	12.2
	(28.1)	(28.3)	(27.7)	(27.6)
R^2	0.73	0.73	0.74	0.72
N	63	62	62	63

Note: Standard errors in parentheses. Coefficient estimates significantly different from zero at the 90 percent (*), 95 percent (**), 99 percent (***) confidence levels.

Hypothesis 4: Ethnic and Regional Differences

Large in-group/out-group differences often lead to policy implementation skewed in favor of one region or group at the expense of others. Many studies have argued that laws and regulations may not be systematically enforced in places that are ethnically, linguistically, or religiously diverse. Ethnographers have shown that national courts systematically discriminate against the poor or members of certain ethnic groups (Starr 1978). In some cases, the identity of incumbent political leaders leads to discriminatory practices or selective implementation of laws against members of other groups.

In other cases, poor enforcement occurs in the interactions between enforcement agents and ordinary citizens. In India, for example, during several episodes of Hindu-Muslim riots, police units received explicit orders from state governors not to intervene when Muslim neighborhoods came under attack by Hindu rioters (Wilkinson 2004). In Lebanon, many private health clinics have been funded by powerful political parties such as the Sunni Muslim Future Movement and the Shiite Hezbollah to serve their coreligionist constituencies. In some neighborhoods of Beirut where most residents are Shiites, the Future Movement has had little incentive to provide health care to the Sunni minority, because the chances of winning the districts in an election have been slim (Cammett and Issar 2010).

To examine this hypothesis empirically, we rely again on the WJP General Population Survey. We look specifically at question 24a, which could be rephrased this way: During the past three years, did you (or anyone living in your household) have to pay a bribe (or money above that required by law) to obtain a government permit, or process any kind of document (like a license, building permit, and so on) in a local government office?

We investigate whether ethnic minorities or individuals in other cities besides the biggest city responded differently to this question. A measure was constructed to indicate whether an individual was an ethnic or religious minority for Egypt, the Islamic Republic of Iran, and the United Arab Emirates based on the ethnicity and religious variables contained in the WJP General Population Survey. For Tunisia, we found only one or two persons who self-reported themselves as minorities, while, for Lebanon, there is no real majority group.

Table 2.10 presents results of probit regressions of a binary variable for whether an individual reported paying a bribe in four of the MENA countries in the sample.[9] We regressed the pay-bribe variable on the ethnic and religious minority variable described above and dummy variables for individuals living in the two nonmain cities (when this information is available) as well as the following control variables: dummy variables for college and high school education (no or low education is the excluded category); a dummy variable for gender (male); a self-perception measure of social and economic condition (sec), which runs from 1 (low sec) to 10 (high sec); age and age-squared; and an indicator variable for whether the individual was a foreigner.

First, the regression shows very strong results for the ethnic minority variable in all three countries where this variable was used in the regressions: Egypt, the Islamic Republic of Iran, and the United Arab Emirates. Table 2.10 provides substantive marginal effects based on the regression results. In row 1, we present the predicted probability that a male age 35, with a high school diploma, living in the largest city, who is not an ethnic minority, and with a medium self-perception of his social and economic condition (sec = 5), would respond that he paid a bribe.[10] In the second row, we present the same probability for an individual who is similar on all counts except that he is an ethnic minority. The three stars next to these numbers signify that the marginal effects are statistically different from the values in row 1 at the 99 percent confidence level.

The substantive results are extremely large. In Egypt, being a minority increases the probability that a male of age 35 (with a high school diploma, and so on) would report paying a bribe by 27.4 percentage points, from a

Table 2.10 Hypothesis 4—Ethnic and Regional Differences

	Egypt, Arab Rep.	Lebanon	Iran, Islamic Rep.	United Arab Emirates
college	−0.316	−0.207	0.455	0.833
	(0.165)*	(0.261)	(0.188)**	(0.567)
high_school	−0.307	−0.081	0.578	0.832
	(0.195)	(0.267)	(0.191)***	(0.535)
male	0.261	0.161	0.118	0.409
	(0.146)*	(0.196)	(0.120)	(0.339)
sec	−0.020	−0.025	0.017	−0.210
	(0.048)	(0.063)	(0.034)	(0.098)**
age	−0.048	0.029	0.113	−0.224
	(0.059)	(0.044)	(0.057)**	(0.087)**
age_2	0.001	−0.000	−0.002	0.003
	(0.001)	(0.001)	(0.001)*	(0.001)**
foreign			−0.554	−0.217
			(0.140)***	(0.401)
ethnic minority	**0.727**		**0.607**	**1.462**
	(0.313)**		**(0.123)****	**(0.360)****
city_2		**−0.610**	**0.692**	**−0.681**
		(0.293)**	**(0.141)****	**(0.339)****
city_3		0.341	0.029	
		(0.603)	(0.169)	
constant	0.753	0.428	−2.837	2.793
	(1.001)	(0.909)	(0.923)***	(1.760)
N	333	216	531	188

Note: Standard errors in parentheses. Coefficient estimates significantly different from zero at 90 percent (*), 95 percent (**), 99 percent (***) confidence levels.

46.3 percent probability for a nonminority to a 73.7 percent probability for an ethnic or religious minority (table 2.11). The effect in the Islamic Republic of Iran is equally strong, passing from 49.3 percent to 72.2 percent; while in the United Arab Emirates, the effect is almost double, passing from 9 percent to 54.6 percent.

Admittedly, this is just one test. Nevertheless, it provides strong support for the hypothesis that ethnic and religious minorities can have different experiences with rule-of-law outcomes in MENA.

Turning to an examination of regional effects, we see that results are not as clear-cut as with ethnic minorities. In table 2.11, rows 3 and 4 present predicted probabilities for the same profile of a male age 35, except that in row 3 he lives in the second-largest city in the country and in row 4 he lives in the third-largest city.

For Lebanon, we observe that if the same age 35 male were living in Lebanon's second-largest city, Tripoli, he would be *less*, not more, likely to report having paid a bribe. By contrast, in the Islamic Republic of Iran, the same man would be 50 percent more likely to report having paid a bribe in the second-largest city, Mashhad. Predicted probabilities for the third-largest city and for the second-largest city in the United Arab Emirates were not statistically different from

Table 2.11 Substantive Regional Effects: Probability of Reporting Paying a Bribe

Ideal type	Egypt, Arab Rep.	Lebanon	Iran, Islamic Rep.	United Arab Emirates
Type 1: Age 35 male, with a high school diploma, living in the largest city, not an ethnic minority, and with a medium self-perception of his social and economic condition (sec = 5)	46.3	80.9	49.3	9.0
Type 2: same as Type 1 but an ethnic minority	73.7***		72.2***	54.6***
Type 3: same as Type 1 but living in the second-largest city		60.5*	75.0***	2.9
Type 4: same as Type 1 but living in the third-largest city		88.8	50.4	

Note: Significantly different from Type 1 result at 90 percent (*), 95 percent (**), 99 percent (***) confidence.

Table 2.12 Rule of Law Summary Table

Hypothesis	Global integrity implementation gap	
1. Political Institutions	*Empirical Support.* Hybrid regimes (measured by the polity2 variable) are correlated with larger implementation gaps. Democratic regimes are correlated with smaller implementation gaps.	
Hypothesis	**WJP General Rule-of-Law Index**	**WJP Factor 6—Regulatory Enforcement**
2. Bureaucratic capacity	*Empirical Support.* Higher income levels (a proxy for bureaucratic capacity) are correlated with higher levels of the WJP General Rule-of-Law index.	*Empirical Support.* Higher income levels (a proxy for bureaucratic capacity) are correlated with higher levels of the WJP Factor 6 measure of regulatory enforcement.
3. Mobilization and collective action	*No empirical support.* No evidence that mobilization and collective action affect the WJP General Rule-of-Law index.	*Empirical Support.* Mobilization and collective action have a substantively significant effect on the WJP Factor 6 measure of regulatory enforcement.
Hypothesis	**WJP General Population Survey–Bribery as a Rule-of-Law Outcome (Q24a)**	
4a. Ethnic differences	*Empirical Support.* Ethnic and religious differences have a strong effect on Rule-of-Law Outcomes	
4b. Regional differences	*No empirical support.* Regional differences have no effect on Rule-of-Law Outcomes.	

those for the respective largest cities. *Hence, we are unable to find systematic differences in rule-of-law outcomes in MENA based on region or location.*

Conclusion

Table 2.12 summarizes findings about the four hypotheses formulated and tested in this chapter. In brief, we find evidence that political institutions, especially the type of political regime, affect the implementation gap, as measured by the

Global Integrity Index. We also find that implementation gaps are smaller with higher incomes, but larger with hybrid regimes than those seen with autocracies or democracies. We find that income as a proxy of bureaucratic capacity is strongly associated with higher rule-of-law scores—both for the WJP General Rule-of-Law Index and for the regulatory enforcement index (factor 6) of the WJP. For collective action, we do not find evidence that it affects the general rule of law, but we do find that it has a substantial effect on regulatory enforcement. As to ethnic and regional differences, we find strong support for the hypothesis that ethnic and religious minorities have different experiences with rule of law outcomes in MENA, but we are unable to find any systematic differences based on region or location.

Notes

1. In addition to these four hypotheses, any serious discussion of the rule of law in the MENA region must take into account the existence of different legal regimes and courts governing some policy areas; for example secular, Islamic, and customary systems of law. This is a very important factor specific to most countries of the region, and a few others in South Asia. The case study on Jordan in chapter 5 discusses these issues in detail, with specific attention to the role of religious courts in enforcing family and inheritance law.

2. For MENA countries, the Global Integrity Index covers six of the seven countries covered by the WJP—Iran is missing—plus 7 more, for a total of 13. The countries, by income categories, are: six lower-middle income (Egypt, Iraq, Morocco, Syria, the Republic of Yemen, West Bank and Gaza); four upper-middle income (Algeria, Jordan, Lebanon, Tunisia); and three high-income countries (Kuwait, Qatar, the United Arab Emirates).

3. Income data were not available for Somalia and West Bank and Gaza, while W-score data were not available for Iraq, and polity2 data were not available for Bosnia and Herzegovina.

4. Autocratic regime, for which polity2 < –5, is the excluded group in this regression.

5. With regressions (not shown) using the autocratic regime (polity2 < –5) variable, the autocratic dummy was not statistically significant either by itself or with the hybrid regime variable.

6. Note that in 2013 Morocco and Libya were classified as hybrid regimes by Polity IV, while Tunisia was classified as a democracy. The rest of the countries continued to be classified as in 2009. http://www.systemicpeace.org/polity/polity4.htm.

7. Because income is an imperfect measure of administrative capacity, the case studies chapters in this volume explicitly bring detailed evidence on the capacity of two agencies responsible for policy enforcement: the tax administration in Morocco (chapter 3), and the customs agency in Tunisia (chapter 4).

8. Data for Jamaica were unavailable in the Quality of Governance; hence, we use GNI data for 2012 from the World Development Indicators. Moreover, the sample is reduced by 1 observation to 96, as cross-sectional data are not available for Hong Kong SAR, China.

9. City data were not provided for Tunisia and as mentioned there are very few ethnic minorities in Tunisia.

10. If we replaced a male with a female, the probability of reporting paying a bribe shrinks by about 5 percentage points in Lebanon, Iran, and the UAE, and the differences are not statistically different from zero. For Egypt, however, a similar age 35 woman would be 10 percentage points less likely to report paying a bribe, and the effect is statistically difference from zero at the 90 percent confidence level.

References

Ames, Barry. 1987. *Political Survival: Politicians and Public Policy in Latin America*. Berkeley: University of California Press.

Bueno de Mesquita, Bruce, Alastair Smith, Randolph M. Siverson, and James D. Morrow. 2003. *The Logic of Political Survival*. Cambridge, MA: MIT Press.

Cammett, Melani. 2006. *Globalization and Business Politics in Arab North Africa*. Cambridge, UK: Cambridge University Press.

Cammett, Melani and Sukriti Issar. 2010. "Bricks and Mortar Clientelism: Sectarianism and the Logics of Welfare Allocation in Lebanon." *World Politics* 62 (3): 381–421.

Cheibub, J. A., J. Gandhi, and J. R. Vreeland. 2010. "Democracy and Dictatorship Revisited." *Public Choice* 143 (1–2): 67–101.

Durand, Francisco. 2003. *Riqueza económica y pobreza política: Reflexiones sobre las elites del poder en un país inestable*. Lima: Pontificia Universidad Católica del Perú, Fondo Editorial.

Geddes, Barbara. 1994. *Politician's Dilemma: Building State Capacity in Latin America*. Berkeley: University of California Press.

Global Integrity Report. 2006–2013. Accessed at https://www.globalintegrity.org /research/reports/global-integrity-report/

Hibou, Béatrice. 2006. *La force de l'obéissance: Économie politique de la répression en Tunisie*. Paris: Éditions la Découverte.

Hicken, Allen, Shanker Satyanath, and Ernest Sergenti. 2005. "Political Institutions and Economic Performance: The Effects of Accountability and Obstacles to Policy Change." *American Journal of Political Science* 49 (4): 897–907.

Levi, Margaret. 1988. *Of Rule and Revenue*. Berkeley: University of California Press.

Levitsky, Steven, and Lucan Way. 2010. *Competitive Authoritarianism: Hybrid Regimes after the Cold War*. Cambridge, UK: Cambridge University Press.

Mares, Isabela, and Mathew Carnes. 2009. "Social Policy in Developing Countries." *Annual Review of Political Science* 12: 93–113.

Marshall, M. G., K. Jaggers, and T. R. Gurr. 2011. *Polity IV Project: Political Regime Characteristics and Transitions, 1800–2011* (accessed January 29, 2013), http://www .systemicpeace.org/polity/polity4.htm.

Morin, Richard. 2013. "Indentured Servitude in the Persian Gulf." *New York Times. Sunday Review*. April 12, 2013.

Moskowitz, Peter. 2013. "Amnesty International: Qatar Failing to Enforce Its Labor Laws" *Al Jazeera*, November 17, 2013.

Przeworski, A., M. E. Alvarez, J. A. Cheibub, and L. Fernando. 2000. *Democracy and Development: Political Institutions and Material Well-Being in the World, 1950–1990*. New York: Cambridge University Press.

Starr, June. 1978. *Dispute and Settlement in Rural Turkey. An Ethnography of Law.* Leiden, The Netherlands: Brill.

Teorell, Jan, Nicholas Charron, Stefan Dahlberg, Sören Holmberg, Bo Rothstein, Petrus Sundin, and Richard Svensson. 2013. "The Quality of Government Dataset." Version December 20, 2013, Quality of Government Institute, University of Gothenburg, Sweden. http://www.qog.pol.gu.se.

Wilkinson, Steven. 2004. *Votes and Violence: Electoral Competition and Ethnic Riots in India.* Cambridge, UK: Cambridge University Press.

World Bank. 2013. *World Development Indicators.* Washington, DC: The World Bank Group.

World Justice Project. 2011. *Rule of Law Index 2011.* The World Justice Project, Washington, DC.

Discretion and Taxability: Enforcing Tax Rules in Morocco

Introduction

This first case study, which analyzes taxation from a rule-of-law perspective in Morocco, was selected for three reasons. First, taxes are central to the social contract between governments and citizens who pay them in exchange for public goods and representation in decision making. Therefore, tax design and enforcement are inextricably linked to political institutions and evaluations of government performance.

Second, more than any other policy area, taxation directly connects the rule of law to economic development. If certain categories of taxpayers' experience unfair treatment in comparison with other groups, or if they lack the institutional channels to challenge a corrupt tax administration, they will attempt to avoid what they perceive to be inequitable taxation. In many cases, these efforts directly impact the investment strategies of firms and the size of the formal sector, with negative consequences for economic growth.

Third, other policy areas are governed by sound formal laws that are consistent with international standards, even though they are often not well enforced. Taxation is unique because it showcases a relatively low gap between laws and enforcement. With few exceptions, no international consensus exists guiding the design of tax laws and codes, the structure of taxes, tax incidence considerations, or who should pay what. By and large, formal institutions in taxation policy tend to mirror the underlying distribution of power in society.

These characteristics of tax policy render it a good candidate for examining the direct link between rule of law and economic development. They are not unique to the Middle East and North Africa (MENA) region and apply in different degrees to advanced industrial democracies as well. However, as argued in chapter 1, the prevalence of autocratic regimes and the lack of institutional checks and balances in MENA place less constraints on governments tempted to use tax policy as a political carrot-and-stick tool for different constituencies of taxpayers.

This chapter examines implementation gaps between tax policy and practice in Morocco. It tests several hypotheses with respect to their political economic causes, and it explores two main findings in greater depth. First, the border between law and enforcement is undefined and permeable, leaving room for the discretionary renegotiation of tax obligations between influential taxpayers and tax authorities. The wide use of tax exemptions, the frequent use of fiscal amnesties and a significant stock of accumulated tax arrears allow for for the "personalization" of tax collection, with negative consequences for perceptions of equity and fairness.

Second, the need to deploy low administrative capacity to collect revenues from sectors that are easier to tax is the most important political economic variable explaining implementation gaps at the micro-level. As a result, large firms, public and private sector employees, and some categories of consumers bear the largest distributive burden of tax policies, a domain where administrative capacity and political incentives intersect.

The chapter has six parts. The "Taxation as Rule of Law in Everyday Life" section argues that taxation is a principal area in which citizens and firms routinely interact with the state and experience the rule of law in practice. In "The Political Economy of Taxation," the chapter reviews the theoretical literature on this topic and proposes working hypotheses. "Pockets of Discretion" presents evidence of implementation slippage in taxation in Morocco. "Political Economic Incentives" attempts to explain why enforcement across taxes and taxpayers varies systematically and analyzes three waves of firm-level surveys conducted in Morocco (2007, and 2013–14) and Tunisia (2013–14). The last section summarizes the main arguments.

Taxation as Rule of Law in Everyday Life

Taxation is a core area of economic policy with wide-ranging implications. It has a direct impact on economic growth and development and it can perpetuate or alleviate inequalities. Politically, tax policy is one of the most tangible manifestations of the social contract between citizens and states. To paraphrase one influential 20th-century economist, the payment of taxes by citizens in exchange for political representation and collective goods "forms the very skeleton of the state, stripped of all misleading ideologies" (Schumpeter 1991). Few policies are in fact more political than taxation.

Revenue collection is also important in the broader sense of rule of law. The majority of citizens and firms interact directly and routinely with agents of the tax administration, arguably more so than with other executive branches of government. The nature of this interaction, coupled with the perception of fairness and equity, may lead to quasi-voluntary compliance, an ideal equilibrium where the state incurs lower costs in enforcing tax codes and taxpayers feel justly treated by the bureaucracy (Levi 1988). Conversely, perceptions of inefficiency, corruption, favoritism, and bias with respect to any aspect of tax collection provoke conflict between taxpayers reluctant to comply with tax laws and a tax administration unable to meet the costs of coercion, ultimately undermining state capacity.

In many countries around the world, tax enforcement is perceived as unfair. Government officials, political leaders, and influential businessmen often manage to avoid paying any taxes in clear violation of the law, leaving the poor to foot the bill. Tax laws themselves are frequently overly complex, opaque, unpublished, and easily broken. Tax authorities are partly responsible for low collection rates and discriminatory enforcement. In several African countries, for example, there is a 40 percent gap between taxes due and taxes collected (Trebilcock and Daniels 2008, 203). In the absence of credible sanctions uniformly applied, tax auditors acting as agents of the government (a political principal) often have incentives to tolerate or take part in corruption. Even when the principal's and the agent's incentives are perfectly aligned, equity and fairness in enforcement can still be problematic. In nondemocratic contexts, tax offices are often more feared than the police, and they assume a de facto repressive role on behalf of the executive, targeting and prosecuting political opponents. For all these reasons, in developing countries "tax administration is in effect tax policy" (Bird and Casanegra 1992, cited in Trebilcock and Daniels 2008, 20).

What are the political economic incentives that lead to the enforcement of tax codes with some categories of taxpayers but not others? The answers come from an analysis of tax policy implementation in Morocco.

The Political Economy of Taxation

Most studies emphasize the distributional choices governments make when designing tax systems. According to a seminal theory, three factors shape strategies to extract revenues: the ability of taxpayer groups to influence the political leaders, the executive's time horizon—or the expected political tenure in office—and the transaction costs associated with taxation (Levi 1988). From this perspective, democracies lead to better policy implementation than autocracies because taxpayers are more likely to comply as long as they perceive their tax burden as fair and predictable. Other studies maintain that the opposite is true: less democratic governments have higher tax collection rates because they are immune to social pressure and have greater coercive power (Haggard 1990). Regardless of the type of regime, the collective action capacity of taxpayers is a key factor determining how tax policies are set and implemented. Vocal demands from business associations, lobbying groups, or influential firms and individuals often translate into concessions in the border zone between policy and implementation. Election cycles have also been found to influence taxation, with rates and enforcement efforts dropping in the runup to elections as politicians court key business constituencies (Cheibub 1998).

Political institutions do not exercise exclusive power over tax enforcement. Economic and administrative constraints also play their parts. Poor states often lack accurate information on the actual tax base and have insufficient capacity to collect taxes. In many countries, tax authorities do not have comprehensive lists of taxpayers, because they lack specialized software, centralized directories, or even correct street addresses.[1]

The ability to tax differs across economic sectors as well. For firms in the service sector, it is easier to hide revenues and increase the costs of enforcement for tax authorities. As a consequence, limited collection capacity is more frequently targeted at sectors that can be taxed more easily, while industries such as real estate and banking go relatively untaxed (Gehlbach 2008).

Some also argue that despite the relatively high administrative costs associated with sophisticated indirect taxes such as the value-added tax (VAT), because they are more widely applied there is a reduced incentive for lobbying that could prevent them from being enforced (Imam and Jacobs 2007, 23).

In general, tax salience, simplicity, and clarity are credited with improving implementation and reducing tax avoidance, although the micro-evidence is somewhat mixed (Finkelstein 2007). Last but not least, when taxes entail multiple direct interactions between tax collectors and firms (for example, taxes on international trade), corruption is more common and enforcement therefore more selective (Imam and Jacobs 2007).

This chapter focuses on Morocco and draws comparisons with Tunisia. It first identifies the general gaps in implementing tax policy, then examines systematic variation in enforcement by type of tax and taxpayer, and considers the political economic factors that may drive these variations. Why, for example, does the tax administration enforce some tax policies more systematically than others? Why do some taxpayers enjoy a privileged position when it comes to tax liabilities and collections? In line with chapter 1, the working hypothesis is that political economic incentives operating within capacity constraints lead to variation in enforcement across taxes and taxpayers. In contexts characterized by weak collection capacity, the tax administration is more likely to deploy its resources toward highly taxable activities and taxpayers,[2] such as large firms, state-owned enterprises, private and public sector employees, and consumer VAT. By contrast, enforcement is lax when it is difficult to tax or when the political economic incentives to settle liabilities on a case-by-case basis outweigh the benefits of systematic tax collection. Table 3.1 summarizes the overall findings, with the caveat that the matrix containing binary placements of taxes and taxpayers serves only as a parsimonious analytical device. In a complex public policy reality, many of these categories would overlap to some extent.

Table 3.1 Varieties of Tax Enforcement by Type of Taxes and Taxpayers

| Capacity | Incentives | |
	High	Low
High	*Corporate taxation*—large firms and (SOEs)	Real estate developers
	Income tax—public and private employees	New exporters
		VAT
Low	*Corporate taxation*—Small and medium enterprises	*Informal economy taxation and formalization*
	Income tax for liberal professionals and independents	

Pockets of Discretion in the Margin between Tax Laws and Implementation

In Morocco, three factors account for a relatively opaque tax policy and make the discretionary treatment of taxpayers possible. First, numerous exemptions have made laws overly complex and difficult to enforce. In turn, this complexity results in increased administrative costs for Direction Générale des Impôts (DGI), the central tax authority, and opens up opportunities for discretionary treatment of firms and citizens.

Second, critics have emphasized shortcomings in revenue transparency. The DGI discloses aggregate data on tax collection and audits by region as well as by type of taxes. Taxes in arrears, however, are not routinely reported, even though they account for a substantial portion of the total stock of taxes payable (Berrada 2012). The lack of data is often the manifestation of negotiations between certain firms and the DGI that enable influential taxpayers to win preferential treatment. A lack of transparency in the management of tax revenues also encourages corruption. While data on tax collection at the national level are generally available, there is a chronic lack of transparency in local taxes. Neither the Direction Générale des Collectivités Locales within the Ministry of the Interior nor the General Treasury releases fiscal data at the commune level, other than in a highly aggregated format, which makes any detailed analysis impossible.[3] Additionally, prebendal forms of collection of "parallel" (informal) local taxes by various local authorities, with or without fiscal mandates, persist in both rural and urban areas, penalizing taxpayers (Akesbi 2015).

Third, tax policy in Morocco has entailed cycles of lax implementation and general amnesties meant to boost compliance in the short run. This cycle ultimately undermines the long-term relationship between the tax administration and taxpayers. This section discusses each of these factors in turn.

Tax Exemptions

Since independence, tax exemptions and reduced tax rates in Morocco have served both economic and political purposes for the monarchy: the formation of a national class of landowners and entrepreneurs, incentives to burgeoning economic sectors, the maintenance of social peace and stability, and an assurance of loyalty from key political and economic actors. Accordingly, these exemptions and concessions benefited elites such as high-ranking military officers and rural notables, as well as broad segments of the population. The exemption of the agricultural sector from income and corporate taxation, initiated in 1984 and gradually phased out between 2014 and 2020, is a controversial example of fiscal policy that favored large farms and rural elites, generating widespread perception of fiscal injustice among urban taxpayers. The exemption of basic foodstuffs from VAT are examples of similar concessions to consumers, a larger pool of constituents.[4]

Beyond these broad arrangements, interest groups managed to secure multiple tax exemptions through intense legislative lobbying (Bensouda 2008). In the agricultural sector, Union Marocaine de l'Agriculture has contributed significantly to securing a privileged fiscal status for its members. In manufacturing and services, the textile and apparel industries, real estate, and the export sectors have been the leading recipients of important fiscal concessions. Figure 3.11 shows the ranking of various economic sectors in terms of lobbying demands formulated during annual budget debates between 1991 and 2015, based on a media content analysis.

Paradoxically, this hedging strategy by the executive aimed at appeasing multiple constituencies simultaneously through tax incentives led to a fiscal version of "the tragedy of the commons." Over time, the increasing number of exemptions eroded the tax base and led to a general incoherence in tax policy, to the point that currently only a small number of readily identifiable taxpayers who can be taxed at minimal cost bear most of the tax burden. In the metaphor of one analyst, the Moroccan tax base came to resemble a Gruyère cheese full of holes (Akesbi 2008, 80). Because tax exemptions are seen as concessions to the political and economic power of certain taxpayers or to the lobbying power of certain groups—agriculture and real estate being the leading sectors—entire categories of taxpayers who are not beneficiaries, especially public sector employees and certain firms, perceive themselves as victims of unfair taxation sanctioned by the law.

Tax exemptions that diminish the neutrality of the VAT have increased the costs of collecting it and raised questions among categories of taxpayers who do not benefit from exemptions. A wide range of commodities and organizations, including food staples such as milk and bread, charitable foundations and agricultural supplies and equipment (primarily for the benefit of the owners of large farms) are exempt from the tax (Akesbi 2008, 76).

At the same time, over the last decades, exemptions have become increasingly unfavorable to lower-income groups. Between 1986 and 2008, VAT on many basic consumer items, including butter, cooking oil, sugar, soap, electricity, and public transportation increased. By contrast, VAT on luxury items such as perfume, electronics, and car engines was reduced, leading critics of fiscal policies to argue that the reforms made the system more regressive while preserving its incoherence (Akesbi 2008, 76). Whereas the VAT accounts for the majority of exemptions, the corporate profit tax is also riddled with loopholes.[5] At the same time, the more systematically enforced income tax has far fewer. This is especially true for the salaries of public and private employees, its largest component.[6]

Until a decade ago, exemptions were evaluated only informally. In 2005, the administration started to more systematically quantify losses from tax exemptions, loopholes, and deductions. Figure 3.3 illustrates progress made in the evaluation of tax expenditures.

By 2011, even agriculture—the most politically sensitive sector—had been scrutinized for revenue lost as a result of special status. The recently formed Social, Economic, and Environmental Council (Conseil Économique, Social et Environnemental du Maroc [CESE]) for the first time published a detailed report on tax expenditures and their incidence by type of tax, economic sector, and beneficiary (figures 3.1, 3.2 and 3.4).[7]

In 2011, tax expenditures totaled Moroccan dirhams (DH) 32.075 billion (or the approximate equivalent of US$3.74 billion). Currently, the VAT—a tax usually associated with high administrative capacity—accounts for 41 percent of the total number of exemptions, most of them the result of the political economic incentives to respond to collective action and lobbying.[8] Firms are the largest beneficiaries of exemptions, accounting for 60 percent of total tax expenditures, followed by households at close to 30 percent.

Two economic sectors stand out in number and amount of expenditures: agriculture and real estate. Agriculture alone accounts for 13.4 percent of the total across all sectors.[9] According to some studies, the state could have collected as much as DH9 billion in income and corporate profit taxes on agriculture between 1981 and 2013.[10] Half of this amount benefited almost exclusively domestic notables who were the beneficiaries of the post-independence redistribution of land (Berrada 2012, 16). Similarly, close to 17 percent of the total amount of taxes the government could raise in the absence of exemptions are related to real estate.[11] Leaving aside the sheer number of exemptions, the laws governing fiscal policy have often been criticized for a lack of clarity that has made it possible to enforce them unfairly. Under the annual budget law for 2008 (Loi de Finances), for example, the VAT rate applied to real estate development activities was increased from 14 percent to 20 percent, but it was never clear if the 6 percent retroactive difference should fall on the developer or the buyer (Akesbi 2008, 75).

Figure 3.1 Tax Expenditure by Economic Sector in Morocco, 2011

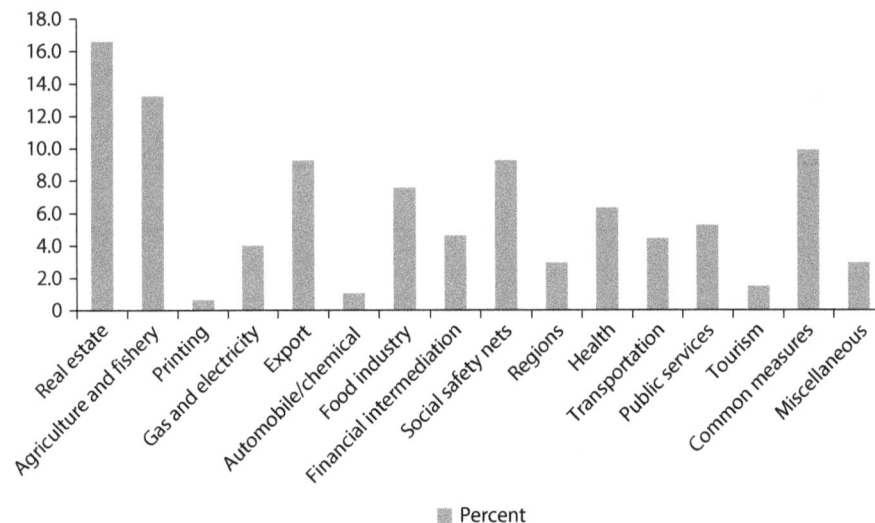

Source: Based on data from CESE 2012, 30–35.

Figure 3.2 Tax Expenditures by Type of Tax in Morocco, 2011
(percent)

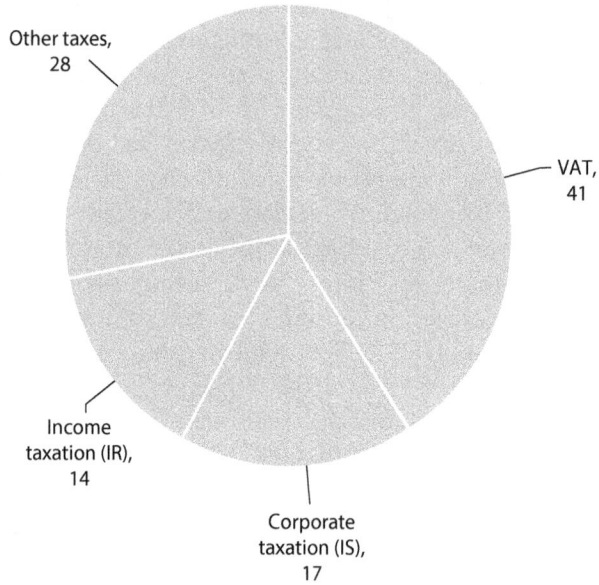

Other taxes,
28

VAT,
41

Income
taxation (IR),
14

Corporate
taxation (IS),
17

Source: Based on data from CESE 2012, 30–35.

Figure 3.3 Evaluation of Tax Expenditures

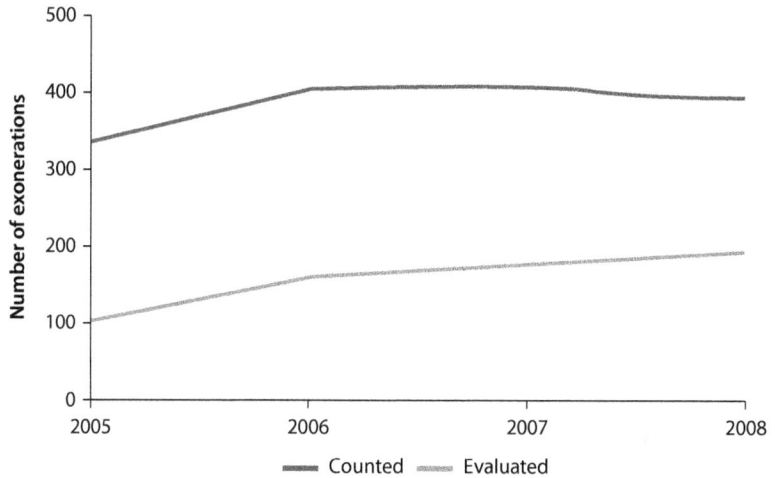

Source: Based on data from TAM 2009, 14.

The Arab Spring ushered in a series of reforms aimed at greater political lib-
eralization, culminating with the drafting of a new constitution in Morocco.
Simultaneously, the 2011 victory of the current ruling party, Parti du Justice
et Développement, an Islamic party with a recent history in the opposition,
signaled a renewal of the social contract between the executive and society.

Figure 3.4 Tax Expenditure by Type of Target Beneficiary, Morocco, 2011

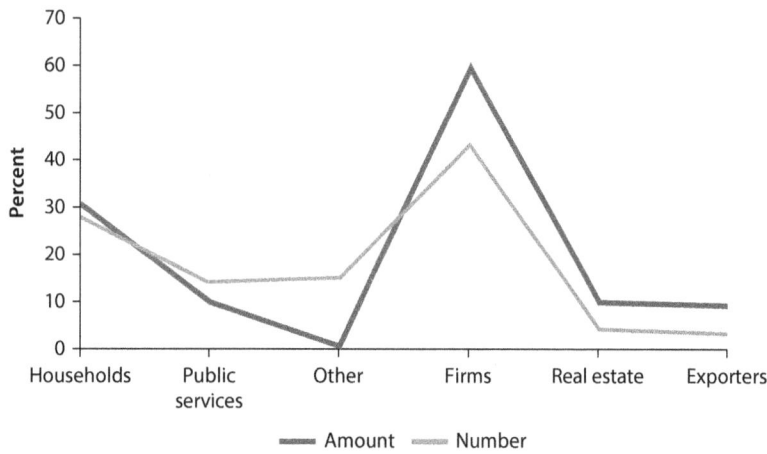

Source: Based on data from CESE 2012, 30–35.

These political developments triggered several concrete steps in the revision of fiscal contracts: a general rethinking of the rent-based economy of long lasting privileges,[12] and the potential taxation of agriculture and greater transparency in tax revenue. Despite gradual improvements in the calculation and reporting of tax expenditures over the last decade, the data are neither fully comprehensive nor methodologically clear yet (Al-Andaloussi 2015).

Tax Arrears

If technically tax exemptions pertain to the formal dimensions of fiscal policy, tax arrears are directly related to policy implementation. There are three common interpretations of arrears: (a) a poor economic climate that weakens the ability of firms to pay taxes; (b) an informal incentive targeting certain firms or sectors; and (c) a discretionary relationship between the tax authority and influential taxpayers whose noncompliance is tolerated. In Morocco, some critics argue that the relatively large stock of tax arrears has been concealed from the public over the years precisely because the largest debtors are high-level officials, members of parliament, or influential businessmen (Berrada 2012; TAM 2009). To illustrate how large a share of tax revenue arrears were in previous decades, in 1993, approximately 9.8 percent of the corporate profit taxes (DH525 million) and 3.8 percent of the VAT (DH265 million) represented the arrears of just two public companies (Berrada 2012, 285).[13] After 2003, as figure 3.5 illustrates, DGI progressively assumed collection responsibilities for the three major categories of taxes and fiscal audits increased significantly, leading to the gradual recovery of around 70 percent of arrears.

Figure 3.6 plots the evolution of the total collection of arrears as a result of tax audits between 2002 and 2010.

Figure 3.5 Evolution of Recovered Taxes, 2003–06

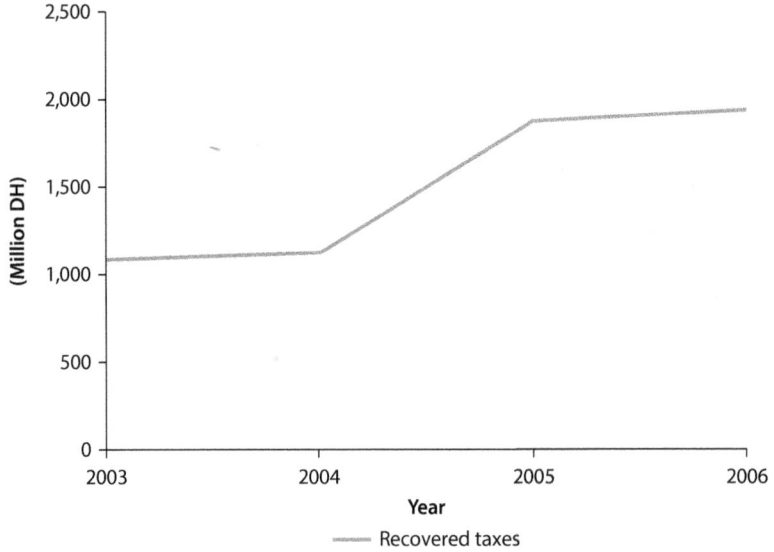

Source: Based on data from Tazi (2008) and Berrada 2012, 279.

Figure 3.6 Rate of Recovery of Taxes Payable, 2002–10

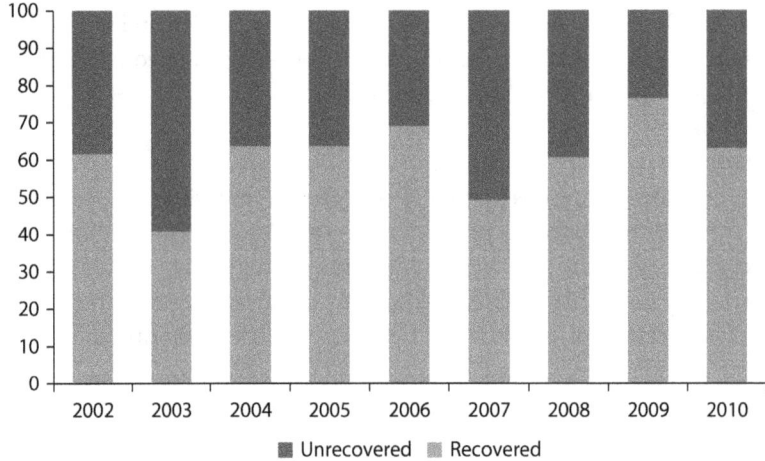

Source: Based on data from Berrada 2012, 291.

Despite improvements, tax arrears still account in part for the gap between tax policy and implementation in Morocco. They lie at the intersection between the administrative capacity to collect and manage revenue, on one hand, and the political economic incentives to elicit taxpayer compliance, on the other hand. Large stocks of declared but unpaid taxes are an indication of the joint influence of both factors and usually a sign of "individualized" negotiations between taxpayers and the tax administration. Moreover, the lack of detailed data on the evolution of the stock and flow of tax arrears significantly reduces the transparency surrounding revenue management.

Several capacity constraints hamper the ability of the Moroccan tax authority to systematically record, control, and report tax arrears. The first institutional evaluation of the DGI, undertaken in 2011 and released in 2013 by the Moroccan Court of Accounts (Cour de Comptes [CDC]), provides some evidence. First, tax collection lacks a coherent strategy. As of 2013, most regional collection units (Recettes de l'Administration Fiscale [RAF])[14] made little effort to elicit compliance on arrears, preferring instead to devote resources to the recovery of current taxes payable. Figure 3.7 illustrates the wide variation in enforcement across four local collection agencies in Rabat and Sale.[15] To give a sense of the scale of the revenue loss resulting from the failure to enforce compliance, in one tax collection agency alone (RAF Laos), total arrears amounted to DH1.346 billion.

Since 2004, when the tax recovery function migrated from the General Treasury to DGI, local collection units have accumulated arrears (*Restes à Recouvrir*) of DH29.6 billion. Even where there are strong incentives to solicit the payment of arrears, long processing delays render collection attempts weak and unthreatening to taxpayers. For example, for liabilities owed in 2004 and 2005, the local collection agency RAF Laos sought their recovery with a delay of two years. Moreover, enforcement was directed at only 3 percent of all accumulated arrears.[16]

Second, the costs of forced collection are not systematically computed and recorded. Consequently, they cannot be included in any analysis. These costs are often manually recorded, without being entered into the central revenue management software (Système d'Information Actuel [SIA])[17] making it more likely

Figure 3.7 Variation in Tax Arrears Recovery across Collection Units in Rabat and Sale

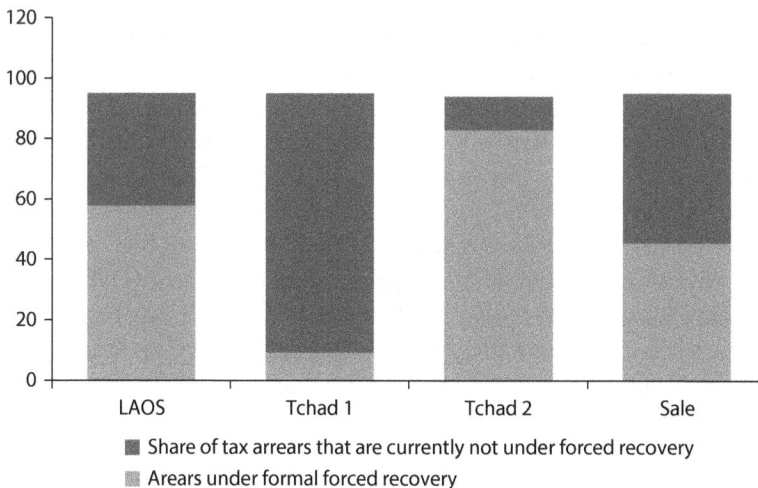

■ Share of tax arrears that are currently not under forced recovery
■ Arears under formal forced recovery

Source: Based on data from CDC 2011, 33.

that they will not be calculated and redeemed from taxpayers as the law requires.[18] The high costs incurred in comparison to the amount in taxes recovered in forced collections often serve as a disincentive for tax agents to pursue them at all. Third, the central software used by the tax administration for revenue management purpose[19] cannot generate quick reports on taxes to be recovered. Even when such data are available, they are often unreliable because of many errors and omissions.

Low administrative capacity makes it difficult to record, analyze, and document the stock and flow of unrecovered taxes in a timely manner. It is therefore impossible to evaluate meaningfully the performance of the tax agency. According to an analysis of fiscal transparency in Morocco, aggregate tax collection data presented by the administration at the end of every fiscal year do not differentiate between types of revenues, that is, whether they represent liabilities incurred and paid during the year or taxes in arrears. Collection agencies (such as RAF) are often understaffed, and many rely on manual systems. Their inadequate capacity detracts from the administration's overall performance. Laterally, collection agencies in different jurisdictions do not exchange information and are therefore unable to identify taxpayers with tax liabilities in more than one place. Collection rates should therefore be interpreted with caution as they might overstate administrative efficiency.[20]

Limited capacity and high costs entailed in collections give incentives to tax agents to focus on large taxpayers and overlook less significant accounts. For example, all of the local collection agencies inspected by the CDC in 2011 devoted efforts almost exclusively to collecting arrears exceeding DH1 million. Small and medium enterprises were systematically overlooked. Moreover, for a large portion of total tax arrears, forced collection never went beyond the notification phase. A similar logic of expedient taxability also applies to local taxes, as DGI often neglects to enforce tax laws in neighborhoods known for low compliance (Akesbi 2008). Section 6 provides supporting microeconomic evidence that the Moroccan tax authority, operating under constraints associated with low administrative capacity, deploys auditing resources toward the largest taxpayers for revenue collection. Easy-to-tax and easy-to-reach revenue sources such as large firms and employees have therefore been the primary targets of enforcement.

The interaction between large firms and the tax administration also entails a crucial political economic dimension. Whereas DGI routinely consults the most influential business associations (for example, Confédération Générale des Entreprises du Maroc [CGEM]) before fine-tuning its enforcement strategies,[21] individualized negotiations regarding payments remain the norm. The prescription of taxes unpaid by some entities is frequent, and the amounts are substantial (DH1.6 billion in Rabat alone). According to the CDC 2011 report, the DGI negotiates deals with large taxpayers without consulting the local collection units. This lack of coordination triggers illegal actions. For example, in violation of the law, accountants with the local collection agencies are sometimes required to adapt to the outcome of the negotiations between DGI and taxpayers and record recent payments against current tax liabilities, not taxes in arrears.[22] In general, the lack of clarity with respect to auditing criteria and the overwhelming settlement of accounts directly with the administration build in an ample space for corruption and political interference (Al-Andaloussi 2015). The "personalized" nature of negotiations between the tax administration and select businesses leaves room for discretionary treatment and leads to suspicion of obfuscation and unfairness. It also signals influential taxpayers that non-coercive options exist, which de facto encourages routine tax avoidance.

Revenue Transparency and Corruption

Transparency contributes to positive perceptions of the rule-of-law status. Conversely, a lack of it or difficulty in accessing and analyzing data raise questions about the equitable treatment of taxpayers and procedural fairness. Leaving aside the problem of tax arrears, revenue management techniques in Morocco suffer from several shortcomings. Critics often point to outdated administrative classifications of revenues, insufficient communication between the tax administration and the public, as well as the lack of basic information on taxes collected by economic sector or by category of taxpayer.[23]

From a rule of law perspective, fiscal transparency and clear communication with the public are essential for dispelling perceptions of inequity and eliciting quasi-voluntary compliance, especially when the budget process is dominated by the executive (Transparency Morocco [TAM] 2009, 8). In recent years, DGI has made greater effort to reach out to taxpayers, communicate more effectively, and improve relations with them through several concrete initiatives, including a 2013 user satisfaction survey and a partnership with business associations for education campaigns meant to induce fiscal citizenship (Al-Andaloussi 2015).[24]

As with tax arrears, some of the less transparent aspects of revenue management stem directly from poor accounting capacity and insufficient coordination among various layers of bureaucracy (DGI, the General Treasury, courts, commercial tribunals, as well as other agencies that deal with tax assessment and property registration, such as Agence Nationale de la Conservation Foncière and local and municipal administrations).

Local collection units (RAF) often fail to scrutinize their accounting methods relating to tax collection. This failure leads to large discrepancies between the data on total collections centralized by the General Treasury and the local accounting records. Given their opaque nature, the deals between the DGI and selected taxpayers are not always accurately reflected in the accounting records at the local level of collection.

Figure 3.8 plots mismatches between General Treasury data derived from reports prepared by the local collection units and DGI centralized statistics. Positive values indicate that the DGI data reflect lower payments than the cumulative reports of local tax authorities.

In corporate profit tax, in 2010 DGI recorded DH2 billion more than the local collection units.[25] While the reasons for the discrepancy are not entirely clear, it is highly likely that the local collection units sometimes mistakenly record in their accounting systems the amounts of taxes negotiated by the DGI and individual taxpayers. Another cause of discrepancies is related to the belated accounting of e-payments (CDC 2011, 34).

Figure 3.8 Discrepancies of Collected Taxes between the General Treasury and the Tax Administration

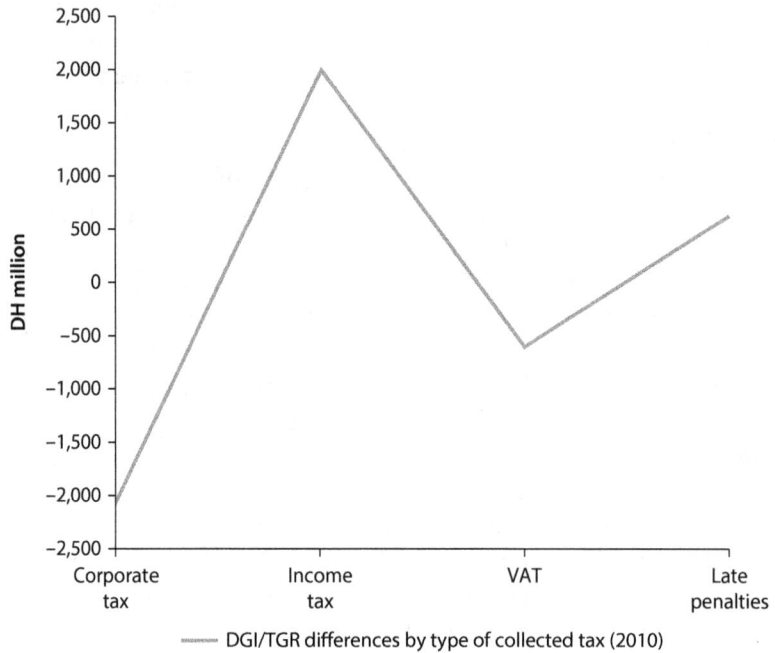

Source: Computed based on data from CDC (2011, 34).

Lack of transparency in revenue management is a two-way street. Because of the limited capacity of the tax administration, particularly in managing the tax base, a majority of small and medium businesses claim losses.[26] Even in the case of large taxpayers, an earlier examination of the tax declarations submitted by 90 Moroccan taxpayers revealed several strategies firms commonly used to avoid taxes. First, they reported lower revenue by deducting anticipated bad debts or shareholder loans. Second, when their capital structure was dominated by debt, they were able to deduct interest from profits. Third, the holding structure of some large private firms made it possible to shift profits to branches or sectors with more exemptions. (Sewell and Thirsk 1997, 339)

Corruption is one of the most serious consequences of a lack of transparency. According to Transparency Morocco, DGI, the tax administration, was perceived as the most corrupt bureaucracy in 2006, with a score of 3.2 out of a possible 5. In 2011, the CDC report drew attention to the weakness of internal auditing mechanisms in the tax administration as well as the underuse of e-payment tools meant to increase the effectiveness of collection and reduce the potential for corruption.[27]

Fiscal Amnesties

Historically, Moroccan governments have frequently used fiscal amnesties as ad hoc measures to compensate for widespread tax avoidance and raise revenues quickly. Three major amnesties occurred in 1984, 1990, and 1998/1999. These fiscal concessions mainly entailed the cancellation of all penalties, fees, and court proceedings contingent upon payment of tax liabilities by certain deadlines. Corporate tax recovery was the most visible target.[28] During the 1990 amnesty, for example, the government's offer involved some 15 taxes. The following amnesty, in 1998, applied to an even higher number of taxes. All penalties, legal expenses, and fines were again waived as long as taxpayers paid their liabilities by December 1, 1998. This amnesty resulted in the recovery of around DH1.3 billion, boosting the collection rate of corporate and personal income taxes by 14.1 percent (Berrada 2012, 285–86, 297; CDC 2011).

Despite meeting revenue goals in the short term, tax amnesties have often proved counterproductive in the long term, because they encouraged lax behavior on the part of taxpayers in default. The expectation of another amnesty proved to be a disincentive for firms to pay taxes on time, as they were able to postpone payments without any penalty until the following amnesty. Furthermore, from a redistributive perspective, the final collection outcomes of the amnesties, in some cases, ended up benefiting a very small number of taxpayers. For example, the 1998/1999 amnesty forgave all tax liabilities incurred up until 1983, and so only a small circle of large landowners and farmers with close relations to the state benefited. Since 2007, measures of this kind have been narrower in scope, aimed primarily at real estate and banking, as sectors notorious for tax avoidance (Berrada 2012, 285–86, 297; CDC 2011; TAM 2009).

In addition to their revenue raising goals, tax amnesties have also been interpreted as political actions undertaken by governments in the MENA region to signal the renegotiation of fiscal contracts between the political leadership and groups of potentially assertive entrepreneurs. In Tunisia, for example, in November 1987, when a bloodless coup transferred power from Habib Bourguiba to Zine El Abidine Ben Ali, a general amnesty signaled the beginning of a new political era (Hibou 2006, 173). In 1995–96 in Morocco, King Hassan II launched a campaign (*campagne d'assainissement*) meant to address the problems of smuggling and the large amount of uncollected taxes (around 50 percent of total taxes payable at the time) (Catusse 2008, 178; Hibou 2004). A newly created commission endowed with significant enforcement powers investigated allegations of fraud, tax evasion, failure to pay import taxes, and abuse of temporary exemptions governing the textile and apparel industry under the *Admissions Temporaires* system (Cammett 2007; Catusse 2008, 178; Hibou 2004). The investigation targeted both large and small businesses and it ended in a general tax amnesty as part of an agreement reached between the government and the business association, CGEM. Under the agreement, firms were exempted from audits for four years in exchange for payment of a turnover tax. Furthermore, in 1998, as a concession to businesses, the government created six commercial tribunals and three appellate courts as a first official platform of interaction between the government and firms (Catusse 2008, 185). Politically, many firms and observers interpreted the campaign as an aggressive attempt by the executive to demonstrate its power to an increasingly assertive business constituency with latent potential to take collective action. The final amnesty led to a resetting of terms, with companies committing to greater fiscal transparency and the administration formalizing the future role of CGEM.[29]

Political Economic Incentives of Tax Enforcement under Capacity Constraints

Aside from the general implementation challenges described above, enforcement varies significantly across types of taxes and taxpayers. This section documents these variations and argues that in general they are driven by pragmatic concerns regarding taxability, as well as by the lobbying power of sector-specific interest groups and taxpayers. In cases such as the VAT and real estate taxes, preexisting capacity to collect is often undermined by political economic incentives that result in lax implementation.

Enforcement Variation across Categories of Taxes

In the last decade, the Moroccan tax administration has focused its efforts on taxes easy to assess and collect, such as income taxes targeting public and private sector employees, corporate taxes from large firms, as well as VAT paid by consumers. Its efforts in these cases have resulted in steady improvements in enforcement capacity. For example, the introduction of an integrated tax management system (Système Intégré de Taxation [SIT]) assigned unique identifiers/numbers to taxpayers.[30] While there is still an insufficient number of skilled users of the system in the regional tax administrations, and despite occasional computational errors,[31] SIT represents an important step in enhancing collection capacity.[32]

The most significant capacity improvements were in areas considered essential for meeting revenue needs. For *corporate profit taxation*, revenue management is more efficient than it is for any other tax.[33] The e-payment system introduced in 2007 for large taxpayers contributed to better enforcement.[34] Two waves of e-tax services (Service des Impôts en Ligne) were launched in 2007 for VAT payment and in 2009 for corporate taxes. The latter received the E-mtiaz Award in 2010. By 2012, according to DGI reports, 3,189 firms started to use these e-portals, leading to a significant boost in corporate tax collection.[35]

Similarly, the *income tax* owed by public and private employees is effectively withheld at the source. In this category, the wages of public and private sector employees are systematically taxed, whereas other taxpayers such as independent professionals are often not subject to declaration requirements and audits. Until recently, the latter constituted a group of professionals with high barriers to entry, restrictive competitive practice, and suboptimal income declarations. The lack of a regular census of notaries, lawyers, architects, and so on diminished the capacity of collection on the side of the administration. Signaling recent political incentives to enforce taxation and boost capacity of enforcement, the Council of Competition released a first comprehensive study of this category in

2013. The DGI followed this signal and launched a systematic campaign meant to correct the underreported income declarations.

By contrast, the application of the VAT and taxes on income and profit in the real estate sector features cases in which capacity gains did not necessarily trigger better enforcement. These cases would fall in the quadrant of high capacity/low political economic incentives of Table 3.1.

The collection and reimbursement of the VAT, commonly hailed as one of the most efficient and high-capacity taxes when judged against international best practice, lacks even basic mechanisms of checks and audits (CDC 2011, 23). Aside from a significant number of formal exemptions associated with the tax, weak control of invoices and manual processing of reimbursements leaves ample room for errors and omissions. For example, several firms with tax arrears were nevertheless eligible for reimbursement. In other cases, companies recovered their claims after long delays.[36] In comparison to other taxes, VAT files are poorly kept, accounts have been lost, and taxpayer databases were incomplete (CDC 2011, 20). In terms of technical capacity, the Moroccan tax administration has made use of SIA, an information system for tax recovery and management, since the 1990s. Not all of the management applications that would make tax collection more efficient are used, however. This is particularly true of the VAT and income tax on real estate profits that, as noted earlier, are riddled with exemptions.

In general, real estate, a sector plagued by rent-seeking opportunities and prone to corruption, is not readily taxable. First, real estate revenues can be easily hidden. According to 2008 estimations, between 15 percent and 30 percent of the value of a real estate property remained undeclared (TAM 2008, 15). This problem coupled with discretionary legal practices that leave tax inspectors ample room for subjectivity when evaluating the real tax base (the controversial ex-article 105 that formally encouraged assessments based on taxpayers' visible signs of wealth, for example) led to a suboptimal tax collection equilibrium and opened ample opportunity for corruption. Recently, the Moroccan tax administration has taken several measures to tackle informal practices and raise additional revenue.[37] Starting in 2015, the introduction of a referential purchase price in 257 areas of Casablanca that sets minimum transaction values as a function of location, type of real estate, and other variables could be an important step toward increasing overall compliance. However, the lack of stakeholder consultations, especially in the case of consumer associations, when designing the referential price may not necessarily lead to quasi-voluntary compliance (Al-Andaloussi 2015).

Second, Moroccan real estate, because of its high profit potential, is the economic sector most exposed to corruption and abuse of political influence (TAM 2009, 4). Undervalued transaction prices for land and problematic public procurement practices favoring market players with strong political ties have been widespread (TAM 2008, 9–19). The strong incentives to either tolerate or collude with noncompliant yet politically influential firms, coupled with severe capacity problems, led to rather subjective and individualized interaction between the tax administration and developers that has eroded formal auditing procedures. As a result, real estate files are often systemati-cally neglected even when auditing capacity exists. According to the CDC, for example, the audit units of certain regional tax offices have routinely elimi-nated real estate developers from target lists and failed to challenge under-stated declarations of income and profits even when evidence indicates as much. Similarly, even when audit capacity existed and the real estate firms were selected for tax inspections, in some cases DGI concluded negotiations with only a partial audit or with none at all (CDC 2011, 26, 38).

Figure 3.9 compares the collection rates across these types of taxes for the last decade. Overall, in the aggregate, income and corporate taxes lead in collection rates, with the domestic VAT lagging behind, confirming the initial hypotheses of this chapter.[38]

Finally, taxation and formalization of the large informal sectors in Morocco is underpinned by an interaction of low political incentives and low capacity of implementation. Numerous and often inconsistent laws governing the informal sector complicate tax enforcement. Analysts argue that the informal sector cannot therefore be considered completely illegal, but is rather a hybrid sector bordering on legality.

At the same time, ties between the formal and the informal sectors, as well as the lack of viable policies that would enable small enterprises to survive if they were incorporated into the legal economy, make policy makers reluctant to take firm action. Because the informal sector offers a means of economic survival for large numbers of their citizens, MENA governments have not made as much effort at enforcement as they might. Taxation of this sector is also a politically sensitive matter, given that the Tunisian revolution was sparked by the

Figure 3.9 Morocco—Collection Rates by Type of Taxes, 2001–11

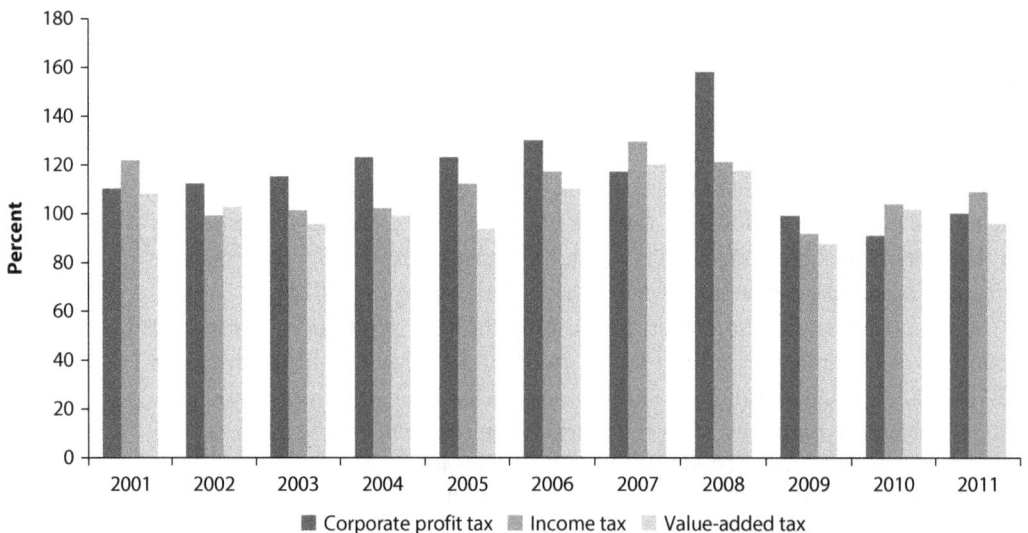

Source: Author, based on data provided by the DGI.

bureaucratic harassment of a street vendor. The Moroccan administration has adopted an ambiguous strategy of alternately strict and lax enforcement in the informal sector, with recent signals of more systematic intentions of formalization. Another constraint limiting enforcement is simply an insufficient number of tax inspectors.[39]

Despite these broad patterns of enforcement across the major tax categories, further analytical disaggregation by type of taxpayer makes a more nuanced assessment of implementation possible. Because of low auditing capacity, efforts to collect corporate taxes are directed for the most part at large firms. A large number of small and medium businesses are only secondary targets of audit as they tend to claim losses or fail to file fiscal declarations at all.[40] Recent exporters, also benefiting from significant tax incentives, are less likely to be audited as well.

Enforcement Variation across Categories of Taxpayers

Auditing is one of the most contentious components of tax implementation. Because it is the most visible interaction between the tax authority and taxpayers, perceptions of the fairness and probity of audits influence judgments of the rule of law in everyday life. Political economic incentives of enforcement, shaped by exogenous capacity constraints, determine targeting strategies.

In Morocco, a heavy reliance on phosphate revenues in the late 1970s led to weak tax enforcement capacity. Prior to the 1986 reforms, the tax administration performed no more than 10 audits a year, when about 200,000 firms were subject to the corporate profit tax, and reached a maximum of 300 investigations for 900,000 households. Furthermore, the collection of income taxes routinely occurred with 15-month delays, causing a loss of up to 5 percent of real tax revenue amid escalating inflation. The administration used multiple identifiers for each taxpayer and did not systematically check consistency.

The underreporting of taxes occurred on a massive scale, with both firms and self-employed professionals engaging in large-scale tax avoidance (CDC 2011). But over time, the administration invested heavily in capacity even while keeping the number of tax inspectors relatively constant, and auditing efficiency improved during the last decade (Figure 3.10 presents the development of auditing capacity).

Despite these gains, auditing decisions and processes are not as transparent as they could be. The 2011 CDC report found that the DGI lacked clear audit strategies and formal ethical criteria for assessing the behavior of tax inspectors. For instance, the accumulation of corporate tax arrears over several consecutive years does not usually trigger the decision to audit. "In fact, all the audit proposals come from tax inspectors based on their individual opinions, which can be subjective" (CDC 2011, 36). The poor management of audit records and the lack of coordination between the DGI and the regional units undermine the auditing process further. Moreover, the number of audits decreased significantly between 2012 and 2013 (Al-Andaloussi 2015).

Recently, the DGI began using specialized software that will eventually enable it to adopt more coherent auditing strategies based on a risk assessment algorithm

Figure 3.10 Evolution of Tax Auditing Capacity in Morocco, 2000–12

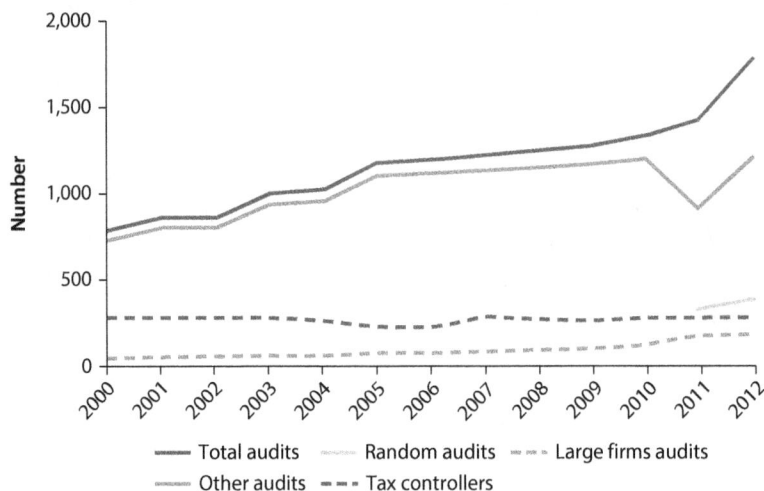

Source: Based on data from and interviews with DGI officials in Rabat, April 2013.

that categorizes taxpayers according to previous tax compliance.[41] Companies with a record of tax compliance will be rewarded with expedited reimbursements. As of early 2013, the DGI had already received several demands from large firms.[42]

Microanalysis of Firm-Level Perceptions of Tax Enforcement

The hypothesis of this chapter is that the need to generate tax revenues under the constraints of low-tax morale renders capacity the driving factor in decisions to audit. The administration is therefore likely to devote its limited resources to auditing large firms and select sectors that are deemed easier to tax. Conversely, it will neglect businesses and sectors where revenues can be more easily hidden, or where there are opportunities to exchange rents, for example in the real estate sector. Empirically, we should be able to see a systematic variation in the pattern of tax inspection or audit targeting.

To test the hypotheses, we analyze three recent World Bank Enterprise Survey conducted in 2006–07 and 2013–14 in Morocco, and compare the results to the benchmark case of Tunisia 2013–14. The respondents were firms selected using a sampling procedure based on three criteria: firm size, sector, and region.[43] The dependent variable of interest is *Tax audit*, coded 1 if the firm was inspected or audited during the previous fiscal year by the tax administration, and 0 if not. The list of independent variables attempts to proxy the hypotheses of section 3. Table 3.2 summarizes the statistical findings regarding the likelihood of a tax inspection during the previous year for three country-level datasets (Morocco 2007, Morocco 2013, and Tunisia 2013).[44]

For Morocco, five independent variables are statistically significant and affected the probability of fiscal targeting inspections at the time of the survey:

firm size, the main market for the firm's products and services, export strategies, geographical location, and type of ownership (public versus private). In 2007, large firms were more likely to be audited than smaller companies.

According to Model 1 of table 3.2, on average, firms with more than 100 employees had a 10.7 percent higher predicted probability of visits by the tax authorities compared to small enterprises. This micro-level finding confirms that given the constraints in auditing capacity (only 224 tax inspectors for all taxpayers in 2006), the DGI focused on large companies to extract revenue more efficiently. This finding echoes recent work on the political economy of taxation in other areas (Gehlbach 2008). For example, following the transition to post-communism, the Russian state focused on extracting from large enterprises that it had had experience taxing in the previous era, leading to a particular type of fiscal contract with large firms in order to facilitate revenue collection.

As a result of this strategy of fiscal targeting, between 2000 and 2012, the total number of audits targeting large firms almost quadrupled, whereas the number of other audits increased by only 63 percent in the same period (see figure 3.10). A close analysis of the years 2005 and 2006, when the 2007 survey wave was

Table 3.2 Comparative Likelihood of a Tax Inspection in Morocco (2007, 2013) and Tunisia (2013)

	(1)	(2)	(3)	(4)	(5)	(6)	(7)
	Morocco 2007			Morocco 2013		Tunisia 2013	
	Tax audits	Tax audits	Tax audits	Tax audits	Tax audits	Tax audits	Tax audits
National market orientation	−0.540 (0.349)			1.262*** (0.483)		0.841 (0.980)	
International market orientation	−0.140 (0.415)			0.767 (0.861)		1.057 (1.009)	
Firm age	0.00606 (0.00821)			−0.0221* (0.0115)		−0.00628 (0.0107)	
Export year		−0.0401* (0.0214)			−0.0765*** (0.0255)		0.0104 (0.0255)
State ownership (%)			0.0207** (0.0100)				
Medium size	0.568 (0.435)	0.501 (0.915)	0.284 (0.857)	0.199 (0.375)	1.842 (1.236)	0.533 (0.335)	0.876* (0.488)
Large size	1.009** (0.461)	1.079 (0.885)	1.406 (0.946)	0.162 (0.625)	1.459 (1.215)	0.768* (0.394)	0.165 (0.574)
_cons	−1.845*** (0.488)	78.41* (42.54)	−2.033 (1.337)	41.83* (22.93)	151.2*** (50.83)	9.564 (21.22)	−23.64 (44.93)
N	447	222	65	371	101	563	269
Model	Logit	Logit	Logit	Logit	Logit	Logit	Logit
Fixed effects-location	yes	yes	yes	yes	yes	yes	yes
Fixed effects-industry	yes	yes	yes	yes	yes	yes	yes

Standard errors in parentheses
***P<0.01, **p<0.05, *p<0.1

conducted in Morocco, also shows that the upward trend continued despite a reduction in the number of tax auditors triggered by a voluntary retirement program. In 2008, for instance, roughly 100 enterprises accounted for more than 80 percent of corporate tax collections, with Maroc Telecom alone contributing DH3.1 billion, approximately 59 percent of all payments from companies that had been recently privatized and 12.5 percent of total corporate tax receipts. The most recent measure taken to institutionalize this targeting strategy was the creation of a Large Taxpayers Unit.

The analysis of the most recent Enterprise Survey wave conducted in 2013–14 in Morocco suggests a potential recent shift toward a more widespread targeting of fiscal enforcement that no longer exclusively relies on a handful of large firms. Firm size loses statistical significance in both Models 4 and 5 of table 3.2.

The most consistent statistical finding that holds for both 2007 and 2013 survey waves in Morocco shows that recent exporters are overall less likely to be inspected by the tax administration. This result is consistent with the third and the fifth theoretical hypotheses put forward in chapter 2, given that exporters are both economically and politically important, thus benefiting from a privileged relationship with the state compared to other firms.

The export-led strategies of growth adopted by many developing countries have placed exporting firms at the top of the list of recipients for fiscal incentives granted by states. New exporters are exempt from corporate taxation and VAT for a significant number of years following the launch of their export activities. Second, the collective action capacity of exporters tends to be relatively high in both lobbying and governance demands. In Morocco, the leading Exporters' Association (Association Marocaine des Exportateurs) has a strong track record of lobbying during the drafting and approval of the annual budget laws. Between 1991 and 2015, for instance, its lobbying efforts reported by the media render it one of the most vocal business associations, after the Moroccan Textile and Apparel Association (L'Association Marocaine des Industries du Textile et de l'Habillement [AMITH]) and the Federation of Real Estate Developers (Fédération Nationale des Promoteurs Immobiliers [FNPI]), two notoriously influential interest groups.

Figure 3.11 ranks 14 sector-specific business associations according to the number of media articles featuring their lobbying demands surrounding the drafting of the annual budget (Lois de finances):

Additionally, recently created exporting firms have been more politically active than old exporters, as several political economy studies have persuasively shown (Cammett 2007; Catusse 2008). A new class of self-made managers of export companies turned out to be an increasingly assertive constituency during the mid-1990s, and managed to secure concrete fiscal gains from the executive.

Table 3.2, Models 2, 4, and 5 show the results of hypothesis testing. On average, in 2013, Moroccan firms whose main products and services targeted national markets were about 18 percent more likely to be inspected by the tax administration than both firms active in smaller local markets and exporters.

Figure 3.11 Intensity of Lobbying Demands and DGI Interaction of 14 Moroccan Business Associations, 1991–2015

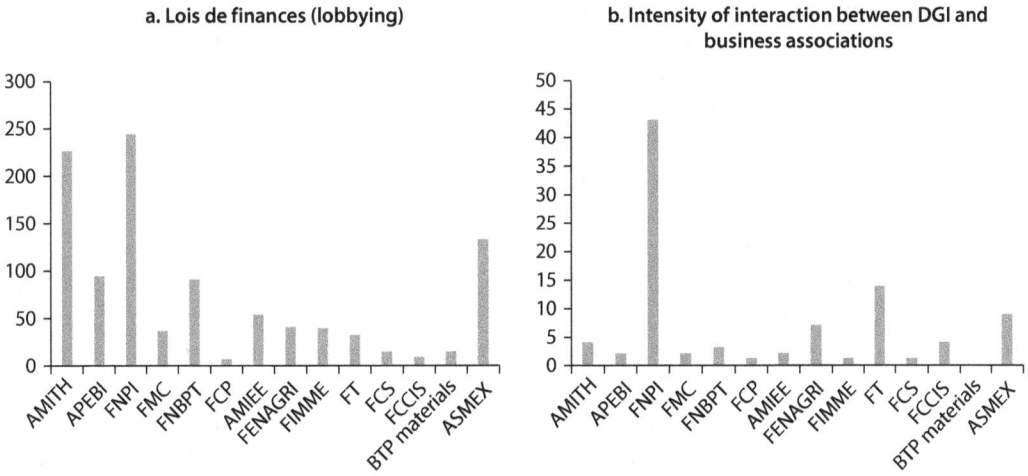

a. Lois de finances (lobbying)

b. Intensity of interaction between DGI and business associations

Source: Content analysis based on 25 Arabic and French language periodicals archived online by Maghress.com.
Note: As took place surrounding the annual budget. AMITH = L'Association Marocaine des Industries du Textile et de l'Habillement, APEBI = Fédération des Nouvelles technologies de l'Information, des Télécommunications et de l'Off-shoring, FNPI = Fédération Nationale des Promoteurs Immobiliers, FMC = Fédération des Industries des Matériaux de Construction, FNBPT = Fédération Nationale du Bâtiment et Travaux Publics, FCP = Fédération de la Chimie et de la Parachimie, AMIEE = Association Marocaine des Industries Électriques et Électroniques, FENAGR = Fédération Nationale de l'Agroalimentaire, FIMME = Fédération des Industries Métallurgiques Mécaniques et Electromécaniques, FT = Fédération du Transport, FCS = Fédération du Commerce et Services, FCCIS = Fédération des Chambres de Commerce, d'Industrie et de Services, BTP materials = Association des Importateurs de Materiel de BTP, ASMEX = Association Marocaine des Exportateurs.

New exporters in particular have been significantly less likely to be targeted by tax inspections compared to older exporting firms in results consistent over time (2007 and 2013). A 10-year difference between the launch of export activities between two firms statistically reduced the probability of a tax inspection by about 5 percent. Keeping all other factors constant, according to two waves of firm level surveys, the Moroccan tax administration seems to show more leniency to newer exporters compared to firms active in international markets longer.

Finally, according to the 2007 survey findings, the tax administration was more prone to inspect state-owned enterprises, although the statistical significance is somewhat weaker and the result more fragile. The marginal change in predicted probability of audit is 0.3 percent for every additional percentage increase in public ownership. This translates into a 30 percent change in the likelihood of an audit if a firm were entirely state owned (Model 3).[45]

The last two results of table 3.2 (Models 6 and 7) test the same substantive hypotheses in Tunisia (2013). With the exception of weak significance for large firms, none receives empirical confirmation. This non finding points at the more randomized selection of firms for tax inspections in Tunisian tax administration, since no category of firms is statistically more likely to be audited than others.

Last but not least, the fourth hypothesis proposed by the empirical chapter suggested that regional differences matter in policy enforcement, for which all three sets of firm-level surveys provide strong evidence. The 2007 and 2013 enterprise surveys sampled across several large urban areas. Figure 3.12 displays the histograms of tax audits by the main regions used to produce the stratified random samples of firms (0 values mean no audit; 1- the firm has been inspected during the previous fiscal year).

In the case of Morocco, being located in the Tanger and Tétouan metropolitan areas (North) significantly reduces the likelihood of a tax inspection for their firms compared to Casablanca, Rabat, or Settat. This geographical discrepancy is also confirmed by the tax collection rates by cities (figure 3.13). Historically, prior to 1956, the year when Morocco gained its independence from the colonial powers, Tangier already had special privileges under international protection. There was zero internal taxation, and the city served as an important commercial entrepôt between Africa and Europe. Its status has also been formally recognized over the last decades. The Free Economic Zone in Tangier, where companies operate under special tax regimes, overall reduces the interference of the tax administration for revenue collection.[46]

Similarly, the geographical location of surveyed Tunisian firms had a strong effect on the probability of tax inspections in 2013. The coastal regions of Northeast and Southwest were around 20 percent more likely to be sampled for audits than Tunis, the capital city.

Figure 3.12 Tax Audits by Geographical Region Sampled in Surveys of Moroccan and Tunisian Firms, 2013

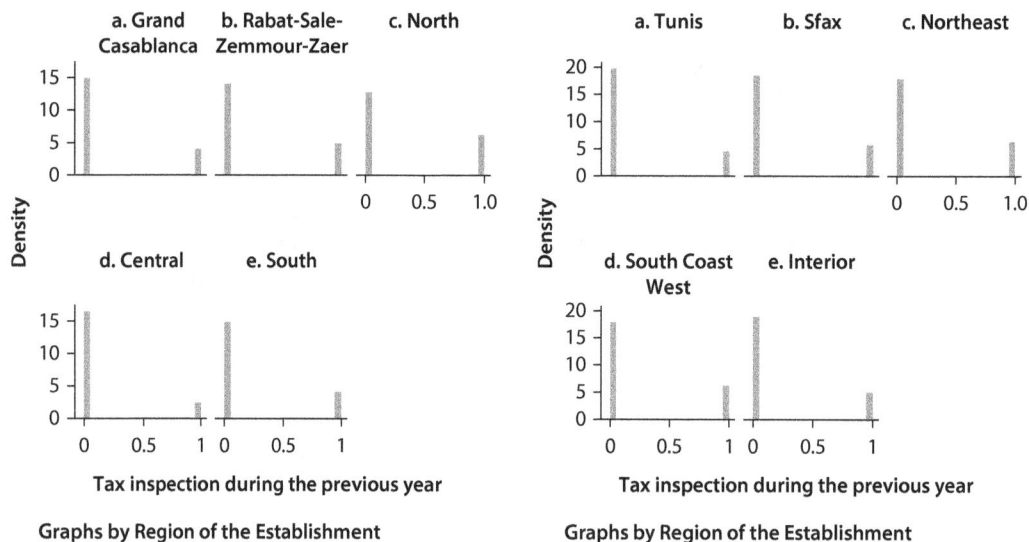

Note: Graphs are by region of the establishment.

Figure 3.13 Corporate Tax Collection Rates, Moroccan Cities, 2006–11

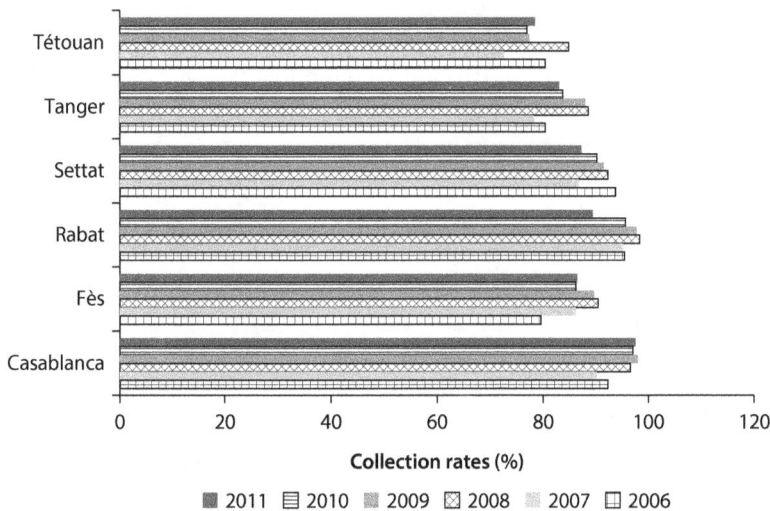

Source: Based on data provided by the DGI.

Taxpayers' Rights

Going one step beyond auditing, the rights and safeguards of taxpayers against the potential abuses of the tax administration are at the core of the rule of law. Historically, there has been no uniform treatment in Morocco. Both procedures and outcomes varied by region, locality, taxpayer, and even tax inspector. The recalculation of taxes often featured different penalties applied to similar firms.

The tax authorities had the legal right to investigate many aspects of taxpayer's finances as well as exercise political pressure under the guise of fiscal audits. Following the 1984 fiscal reforms, a routine audit could take up to 10 years to complete. The 1997 annual budget law reset the limit on how long an audit could go on and how long the National Commissions of Fiscal Recourse (Commissions des Recours Fiscal) could take to reach a verdict. Another important legislative step came in 2005 with the Code of New Fiscal Procedures that introduced additional guarantees for taxpayers. The rate of appeals examined by the National Tax Commission increased significantly in only two years, from 50 percent in 2005 to about 99 percent in 2007 (PEFA 2009, 25–29).

The most controversial form of administrative interference has been the tax inspectors' discretion to perform a general assessment of the entire financial condition of the targeted entity during the course of an auditing process (*l'Examen de l'Ensemble de la Situation Fiscale*). Auditors, acting alone, were able to question and reject the balance sheet and the accounting methods a firm used. Moreover, the practice was never clarified by any supplementary acts or implementation notes between 1993 and 2005. Despite the tax administration's pledges to refrain from legal abuses, the 2005 code maintained the extra-accounting logic of audits, allowing tax inspectors a significant margin of discretion (Elbacha 2006).

In 2011, in line with the political challenges associated with the Arab Spring, and following the demands of two influential business associations (CGEM and FNPI), a new Chart of the Taxpayer was drafted, marking a positive development in de jure safeguards against administrative interference.[47] The new stipulations impose a four-month limit on deliberations for the Local Tax Commissions and nullify the audit notification if the tax inspectors fail to send the Chart to the taxpayer concerned. Despite de jure progress, the 2011 report of the Court of Accounts still noted the administrative abuses that the extra-accounting auditing methods permit.

Conclusion

This chapter analyzed tax policy enforcement in Morocco based on the theoretical hypotheses formulated in chapter 1. It asked three questions: first, is there an implementation gap between tax laws and practice? Second, are there any systematic differences in enforcement across categories of taxes and taxpayers in Morocco?

The answers to the first question suggest that most implementation slippage occurs at the intersection between policy and actual application. In that sense, the gap has been relatively small, as the laws and regulations themselves allowed variation of treatment across taxpayers. Three main practices have generated opportunities for discretionary behavior and personalized the relationship between taxpayers and the tax administration: numerous exemptions, arrears, and the use of fiscal amnesties.

Tax exemptions, a result of collective action/lobbying efforts of firms from a few sectors (agriculture and real estate leading on this indicator), have eroded the tax base, decreased revenue management transparency, and created widespread perceptions of unfairness.

Accumulated arrears opened the door for direct negotiations between the administration and some firms, a process that has raised doubts in terms of procedural equity and equal treatment before the law. The negotiations with the administration are also prevalent because of distrust in courts as alternatives for fiscal dispute resolution.

Finally, the repeated use of fiscal amnesties either ended up benefiting a small number of companies or entrapped firms in a low equilibrium of expectations with respect to future tax collection.

In recent years, the Moroccan government and tax administration have started to tackle some of these challenges. Tax expenditures have become increasingly transparent, fiscal amnesties are more rarely used and target specific sectors only, and there has been notable improvement in the collection of arrears.

The second question followed the research design presented in chapter 1 to explore the reasons for variation in tax enforcement across *specific categories of taxes and taxpayers*. The chapter used both macro- and micro-level evidence to test three main hypotheses that help place taxes and taxpayers in the four quadrants of table 3.1: (a) administrative capacity to collect taxes and reach taxpayers; (b) political incentives to enforce certain taxes based on collective action potential and lobbying; and (c) incentives to enforce or not based on the importance of the firms or sectors in the Moroccan economy.

Hypotheses b and c are confirmed. Even in cases of relatively high administrative capacity to collect taxes, discretionary enforcement results from political economic incentives. This is the case of VAT taxes, eroded by exemptions, whose management and reimbursements are still driven by idiosyncratic considerations related to the taxpayer, diminishing efficiency in collection. Real estate developers also fall within the high capacity—low incentives quadrant (table 3.1), as they combine opportunities for easy-to-hide revenue and high rent-seeking opportunities. For both economic and lobbying influence considerations, new exporting firms seem to be less audited on average than older exporters. As a result, to maximize revenue under the constraints posed by a low collection capacity, the Moroccan administration has primarily deployed its resources toward taxable activities (large firms, state-owned enterprises, income tax on wages) (quadrant 1 of table 3.1).

In some cases, such as small and medium size enterprises or income tax for independent professionals (quadrant 3 of table 3.1), exogenous capacity constraints have been the primary factor behind lower levels of enforcement. Finally, although not directly tested in the chapter, the informal economy lies at the intersection of low capacity and low political economic incentives to enforce taxation because of latent collective action potential (quadrant 4 of table 3.1). In 2013, the government restarted gradual formalization and initiated national consultations, the results of which are still to be seen.

In conclusion, this chapter used both macro- and microeconomic evidence to investigate tax enforcement in Morocco. Whereas bureaucratic discretion still plays an important role in the relationship between the administration and taxpayers, the Arab Spring brought some undeniably positive changes. In Morocco, under conditions of political competition and a shifting fiscal contract, many tax expenditures have started to be evaluated, CDC for the first time has published an audit of the tax administration, fiscal amnesties are used less and less, and fiscal inequities related to agriculture and the rent economy have started to be openly addressed. Importantly, the recent Code of Taxpayer Rights formalized the limits of discretion the administration can exercise.

Notes

1. In Morocco, local tax collection agencies often have a high return rate of notifications sent to taxpayers because of incomplete or wrong address.

2. Taxability refers here to the anticipated tax compliance of different economic sectors, or the relative difficulty of firms to hide revenue from the state (Cheibub 1998; Gehlbach 2008, 63; Levi 1988).

3. Direction Générale des Collectivités Locales is a unit of the Ministry of the Interior; the General Treasury is the Trésorerie Générale du Royaume.

4. Starting in 1984, agriculture has benefited from a special status, exempt from all income and corporate taxation. Despite the fact that this status has been phased out since the beginning of 2014, temporary tax reductions will still benefit the large majority of farms until 2020.

5. In 2008, for example, the corporate tax had seven different rates for 44 categories of beneficiaries (Akesbi 2008).

6. The income taxes on salaries are withheld by employers compared to other types of income subject to different declarative regimes. Salary taxation takes up around 76 percent of all income tax. In 2003, out of 2.6 million Moroccan taxpayers, 2.3 million were employees (Akesbi 2008).

7. Figures 3.2–3.5 are based on data from CESE 2012, 30–35, and data published in TAM 2009, 14.

8. Between 1986 and 2010, 132 amendments modified the initial VAT law. This share already corresponds to a streamlined and much simplified VAT compared to its previous applications. This process has led to the elimination of many exemptions and to the reduction of three separate rates. Between 2006 and 2009 alone, the total number of exemptions was reduced by 64 measures, accounting for DH6.6 billion.

9. According to the CESE 2012 assessment, agriculture alone accounts for 23 percent of the tax expenditures associated with the income tax, 4 percent of the corporate profit tax, and 16 percent of the VAT.

10. TAM 2009, 16. The CESE 2012 report evaluates around DH4.3 billion.

11. Real estate is a major economic sector in Morocco, accounting for approximately 7 percent of GDP employment. Despite its role in the economy, it has been characterized by rent-seeking and severe lack of transparency.

12. For the first time since independence, the Ministry of Transport and Equipment, to enhance transparency in public procurement and incorporate these firms and individuals into the tax base, publicly released the lists of beneficiaries of exploitation permits for sand quarries. Traditionally, this sector has provided significant economic rents and was dominated by notables with high-level political connections.

13. SA Marocaine de l'Industrie du Raffinage and Office National des Postes et Télécommunications.

14. RAFs associated with the regional tax offices Directions Regionales des Impôts.

15. The indicators refer to tax arrears not collected for more than four years.

16. DH22 million out of a due total of DH715 million (CDC 2011, 32).

17. SIA, developed in 1993, has been used in parallel with the more recently introduced SIT.

18. Article 91 of the Tax Recovery Code— *Code du Recouvrement* (CDC 2011, 32).

19. SIA (CDC 2011, 31)

20. This computational problem was mentioned for the first time in the 1980 audited annual budget (*Lois de Reglement*) (Berrada 2012, 281).

21. Based on interviews with DGI officials, March 2013, Rabat.

22. This procedure breaches article 27 of the Tax Recovery Code (*Code du Recouvrement*), CDC 2011.

23. For example, it is not easy to find information on the distribution of income taxation across salaries and other professional earnings.

24. Interviews with DGI officials, Rabat, March 2013.

25. For the tax collection agency from Casablanca Rachidi, the Recettes á Classer [RAC] amount reached DH1.7 billion in 2011.

26. In 1977, 38.8 percent of all firms declared losses; in 1982, 46.7 percent; in 1985, 54.5 percent, and in 2012, 64 percent (Berrada 2012, 293–94).

27. After two years, only 60 companies have used the e-payment system to pay taxes. There is a large discrepancy between the number of e-payment users reported by the DGI and by the 2011 CDC audit report.

28. In 1999, corporate profit taxation accounted for 60.2 percent of the total recovered after the general amnesty.

29. IMF Board of Directors, EBM/96/109-12/6/96: 40.

30. SIT entailed two parallel systems: *SIT Assiette* for the management of the tax base, and *SIT-PVRC* for fiscal control and audit. Even though the integrated software system was supposed to be fully implemented by 2009, the CDC report documented large delays even in the pilot sites that had priority in project implementation. Three years after the initial deadline, the final version of the SIT was still pending (CDC 2011, 44).

31. The SIT cost over DH100 million between 2003 and 2009. Overall, the CDC 2011 report emphasized a general lack of trust and reliability of the integrated tax information system despite its high costs of implementation.

32. For example, some system users changed the rules of tax liabilities calculations in the absence of any changes in the fiscal legislation (CDC 2011, 43–45).

33. Two-three month delays in the process of recording tax payments still persist (CDC 2011, 22).

34. Based on interviews with DGI officials, Rabat, April 2013.

35. Based on interviews with and data collected from DGI officials, Rabat, April 2013.

36. Berrada 2012, and interviews with academics, Rabat, April 2013.

37. For example, the administration reported a significant increase in the profit taxes collected from the real estate sector between 2006 and 2007.

38. The only notable exception is 2009, when the economic crisis led to a lower yield of the corporate tax. The boost in the VAT rates allowed the administration to compensate for this temporary decrease.

39. Many informal firms already pay the business tax (*la patente*) in Morocco. Hibou (2006), Catusse (2008), Majaati-Alami (2008), interviews with academics and politicians in February 2009 and April 2011, Rabat.

40. Some estimates suggest that up to 60 percent of firms declare losses and up to 40 percent never file tax declarations (CDC 2011).

41. Classic audits used to take between 6 and 12 months for large corporate accounts.

42. Based on interviews with DGI officials, March 2013.

43. Since the survey does not comply with the Enterprise Survey's global sampling strategy, the generalizability of the results for the entire population of Moroccan firms for the 2007 survey wave should be approached with caution. In contrast, the 2013 wave is nationally representative for Morocco and Tunisia of a population of over 14,000 and 16,000 firms, respectively.

44. The two consecutive survey waves for Morocco did not solicit responses from the same firms, thus limiting the statistical analysis of the two datasets. The results are presented as logit coefficients (log odds ratios). For the major findings, the changes in predicted probabilities are also computed and included in the text.

45. The sample of firms with significant public ownership is too small to generate statistical confidence in this finding.

46. The number of firms operating in the area expanded rapidly from 23 in 1999 to 522 in 2012.

47. Interviews with DGI officials, Rabat, April 2013, and various media reports.

References

Akesbi, Najib. 2008. "Une Fiscalité Complexe, Incohérente et Injuste." *Études et Sondages. La Revue Economia* 3: 73–92.

———. 2015. "Transparence, Rente et Justice Fiscale." *La Revue Economia* 24: 42–47.

Al-Andaloussi, Driss. 2015. *Rapport de Diagnostic: Transparence et Gestion Fiscale au Maroc*. Rabat: Transparency Morocco.

Bensouda, Noureddine. 2008. *Analyse de la Décision Fiscale au Maroc*. Casablanca: La Croisée des Chemins.

Berrada, Abdelkader. 2012. "Politique Fiscale et Déficit Persistant de Transparence et de Performance." *REMA: Revue Marocaine d'Audit et de Développement* 33: 273–98.

Bird, Richard, and Milka Casanegra. 1992. *Improving Tax Administration in Developing Countries*. Washington, DC: International Monetary Fund.

Cammett, Melani. 2007. *Globalization and Business Politics in Arab North Africa: A Comparative Perspective*. Cambridge, UK: Cambridge University Press.

Catusse, Myriam. 2008. *Le Temps des Entrepreneurs? Politique et Transformations du Capitalisme au Maroc*. Institut de Recherche sur le Maghreb Contemporain. Paris: Maisonneuve & Larose.

CESE (Conseil Economique, Social et Environnemental du Maroc). 2012. "Le Système Fiscal Marocain, Développement Économique et Cohésion Sociale." Rabat: Royaume du Maroque.

Cheibub, Jose A. 1998. "Political Regimes and the Extractive Capacity of Governments: Taxation in Democracies and Dictatorships." *World Politics* 50 (3): 349–76.

(CDC) Cour des Comptes. 2011. *Direction Générale des Impôts*. Rabat: Rapport Annuel.

Elbacha, Farid. 2006. *Les Procédures de Taxation et de Verifications Fiscales: Quelles Garanties pour les Contribuables?* Rabat: Centre Marocain des Études Juridiques.

Finkelstein, Amy. 2007. "E-ZTax: Tax Salience and Tax Rates." National Bureau of Economic Research: Unpublished manuscript.

Gehlbach, Scott. 2008. *Representation through Taxation: The Political Economy of Postcommunism*. Cambridge, UK: Cambridge University Press.

Haggard, Stephen. 1990. *Pathways from the Periphery: The Politics of Growth in the Newly Industrializing Countries*. Ithaca, NY: Cornell University Press.

Hibou, Béatrice. 2004. "Fiscal Trajectories in Morocco and Tunisia." In *Networks of Privilege in the Middle East: The Politics of Economic Reform Revisited*, edited by Steven Heydemann, 201–22. New York: Palgrave Macmillan.

Hibou, Béatrice. 2006. *La Force de l'Obéissance: Économie Politique de la Répression en Tunisie*. Paris: Éditions la Découverte.

Imam, F. Patrick, and Davina A. Jacobs. 2007. "Effect of Corruption on Tax Revenues in the Middle East." Working Paper 07/270. International Monetary Fund, Washington, DC.

Levi, Margaret. 1988. *Of Rule and Revenue*. Berkeley: University of California Press.

Mejjati Alami, Rajaa. 2008. "Comment Définir l'Informel? Derb Ghallef: Le Bazar de l'Informel." *Études et Sondages. La Revue Economia* 2: 80–94.

———. 2009. *Maroc—Rapport sur la Performance de la Gestion des Finances Publiques (PEFA): Evaluation des Systèmes, des Processus et des Institutions de Gestion des Finances Publiques du Maroc*. Washington, DC: World Bank.

Schumpeter, Joseph A. (1991). "The Crisis of the Tax State," In *The Economics and Sociology of Capitalism*, NJ edited by Richard Swedberg, 99–140. Princeton, New Jersey: Princeton University Press .

Sewell, David, and Wayne Thirsk. 1997. "Tax Reform in Morocco: Gradually Getting It Right." In *Tax Reform in Developing Countries*, edited by Wayne Thirsk, 329–60. Washington, DC: World Bank.

TAM (Transparency Morocco). 2008. "La Nébuleuse du Foncier et de l'Immobilier." *Transparency News* 3: 9–20.

TAM. 2009. "La Transparence dans la Gestion des Recettes Fiscales." *Transparency News* 8: 6–16.

Tazi, Ahmed. 2008. "Lutte contre la Fraude Fiscale: Le Renforcement de la Qualité du Contrôle Fiscal." *Revue Française de Finances Publiques* 102: 78.

Trebilcock, Michael J., and Ronald J. Daniels. 2008. *Rule of Law Reform and Development: Charting the Fragile Path to Progress*. Northampton, MA: Edward Elgar.

World Bank. 2007/2013. *Enterprise Survey (Morocco and Tunisia)*. Washington, DC: World Bank.

CHAPTER 4

Discretion and Good Practice: Enforcing Customs Regulations in Tunisia

Introduction

Customs services play an important role in every economy because they perform wide-ranging functions, from trade facilitation, collecting revenues, and combating fraud to boosting security by preventing the import of weapons and narcotics and protecting consumers by confiscating potentially harmful counterfeit goods. Revenue collection is a crucial customs function in many developing countries. Tunisia is no exception, with customs revenues accounting for about 25 percent of the country's total revenues.

This chapter applies the conceptual framework for the enforcement of the rule of law (as presented in chapter 1) specifically to customs administration, and uses the Tunisian customs as a case study. It shows that Tunisia's customs reforms in line with international good practice have been stymied by discretionary and selective enforcement of what on paper are generally good rules and regulations. This implementation gap seems related to some political institutional variables already identified in chapter 1, such as a lack of accountability of customs officials, weak monitoring of their activities, weak or misaligned incentives, and entrenched rent-seeking practices.

The first section of this chapter describes important legal and regulatory reforms in Tunisia's customs service implemented from 2009. Evidence of the discretionary implementation of rules and regulations regarding trade facilitation and the custom service's fight against fraud and corruption is presented in the next section. The third section traces the root causes of the gap between reforms on paper and their actual enforcement, and looks at the effect of internal accountability relationships and the staff incentives. The final section looks at the effect of this enforcement gap on the custom service's performance and concludes.

Customs Legal Reforms

The Tunisian customs service was placed on a new footing in 2009 with the adoption of major legal and regulatory reforms to strengthen economic competitiveness and enhance protections for users. The country wanted to become party to the revised Kyoto Convention[1] on the simplification and streamlining of customs procedures and was ready to revise its customs code to do so. The Tunisian government believed that by aligning regulations with those of its principal trading partners, it could attract more foreign investment. Accordingly, Tunisian authorities took steps toward adopting international good practices based on the recommendations of the World Customs Organization (WCO).[2]

The reforms had three overriding objectives: facilitating trade, fighting corruption through greater automation, and promoting professional integrity. Key global concepts were integrated into the new customs code; among them customs valuation and the definition of "origin."[3] Tunisian customs also introduced the principle of "transaction value" as a basis for customs valuation.[4]

Trade Facilitation through a Revised Risk Analysis System and Simplified Procedures

The Tunisian customs service, with facilitation of trade as a main objective, adopted an array of reforms focused on risk analysis and new regimes that waived customs duties.

Risk analysis is a key mechanism in customs operations in Tunisia that rely on a system of alternative channels. Although computerized data processing was introduced as early as 1982, risk analysis was not automated until 2004. Controls and the selection of cargo for inspections had been largely subjective and were not based on risks. In 2004, a three-channel system (green, orange, and red) was introduced to simplify and expedite customs clearance.[5] Goods passing through the green channel would not require any control, while a paperwork control would be required for goods through the orange channel. Only the red channel would entail physical inspections. The choice of channel is based on a scoring methodology that takes into account the nature of the goods, their country of origin, their destination, and their value. In addition, some declarations could be randomly assigned to the red channel, while some importers could be exempt from scoring altogether.

Official figures indicate that most imports pass through either the green or the orange channel (that is, without a physical inspection), but this figure may be inflated since it includes exports and empty containers. In 2009, 59 percent of goods passed through the green, 21 percent through the orange, and 20 percent through the red channel. In 2010, these figures were 48, 41, and 11, respectively (figure 4.1).

Along with the enhanced risk analysis system and in line with promoting information exchange between all customs actors, Tunisia sought to strengthen the customs-to-enterprise relationship. before the 2009 reforms, the investment

Figure 4.1 Breakdown of Customs Declarations by Color Channels in 2010
(percent)

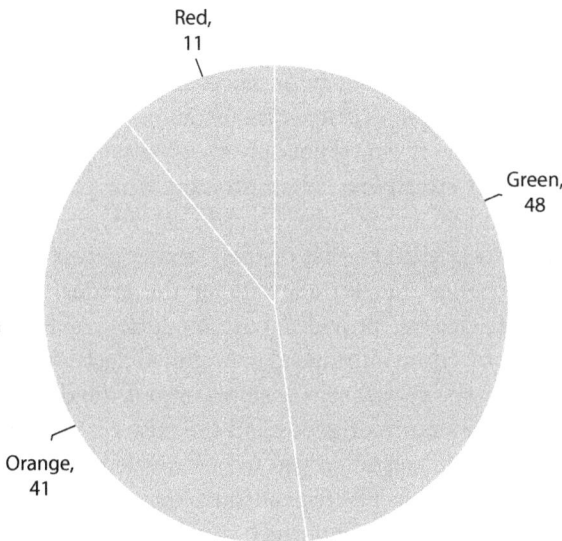

Source: Tunisian Customs.

code distinguished between "fully exporting" and "partly exporting" enterprises, commonly referred to since 1972 as "offshore" and "onshore" enterprises.[6] Fully exporting firms benefited from a range of tax exemptions for their first decade in business, including exemptions from profits, export and import taxes, as well as from value added tax.[7]

Starting in 2009, some regimes permitting a waiver of duties were introduced, with the aim of boosting trade. Several of these exemptions regimes are based on the intended use of the imported goods. The most basic, known as "Temporary Admission" (Articles 233–242 of the Tunisian customs code), exempts from taxes goods imported for temporary use on Tunisian territory. This reform also improves transparency by specifying the conditions that must be met to benefit from Temporary Admission, and by detailing the criteria for total or partial exemption. For instance, imported goods deemed beneficial to the national economy, such as primary materials and machinery needed for public works projects, can fall under this regime, and so can goods considered "sporadic and individual," provided that their exemption does not significantly reduce public finances. In all cases, customs officials must approve exemptions case by case. Another regime introduced in 2009 concerns the transit of goods. It allows the transport of foreign goods through Tunisian territory, and transfer between two warehouses, without any taxes or duties. Most of the declarations under the transit regime concern goods transiting between ports and warehouses.

In keeping with international practice and to meet WCO requirements, Tunisia created the legal status of "Authorized Economic Operator" in 2009.[8]

This label aimed at strengthening relations between the customs service and businesses. It was touted as one of the most meaningful customs reforms because it provided for anticipated clearance, automatic passage through the green channel, simplified procedures, and the least-burdensome guarantees, such as a partial flat fee guarantee or a global annual guarantee. Apart from a minimum required output, applicants needed only to be in good standing with customs, the tax administration, and the social security administration to be eligible.

The reforms of 2009 were aimed not only at diversifying customs regimes, but were also intended to streamline administration. The procedures facilitation committee (comité de facilitation des procédures) was formed, and two new procedures were introduced. The first of these, the initial estimated declaration (déclaration initiale prévisionnelle) allowed for the gradual removal of goods once they had been cleared, provided custom duties were paid within one month. The second procedure introduced a simplified declaration, making it possible to physically remove goods from customs even if the declaration is incomplete, provided that the nature of goods and the customs regime were defined. In both cases, a complete declaration was to be provided within eight days.

Moreover, the 2009 reforms relaxed constraints on trusted importers by introducing anticipated procedures. Importers could use an anticipated manifest (Article 80 of customs code) or an anticipated customs declaration (Article 100 of customs code) to secure a customs clearance before goods arrived. At the same time, all fully exporting and some partly exporting firms, including oil and gas companies, could benefit from the immediate clearance of goods provided a guarantee was paid and, if need be, the declaration could be updated within eight days.

Fighting Fraud and Corruption through Automation and Promoting Integrity

The fight against corruption and the promotion of integrity was another overarching goal of the 2009 reforms. Corruption in customs typically takes the form of tax evasion, which could include: (a) underreporting of unit value, (b) underreporting of taxable quantities, (c) a misclassification or wrong declaration of tariff lines, to benefit from lower duties applied, and (d) smuggling (Mishra, Subramanian, and Topalova 2008). Customs fraud and tax evasion are typically mitigated by the automation of procedures and data management systems that cut down the interactions between customs officers and traders, thereby reducing opportunities for bribery and extortion.

According to the third article of the Tunisian customs code, three key documents were made available in electronic format: the summary declaration (the manifest), the detailed declaration, and the simplified declaration. Electronic signatures were also accepted, and electronic payments of taxes and duties were also made possible, at least in principle.

The Tunisian Customs Data Computing System SINDA (Système d'Information Douanier Automatisé) is generally considered the cornerstone of the customs service's fight against corruption. Although officially launched in May 1977, the system only started to be used in 1982. It became truly efficient and automated in 2004, when it was finally possible to conduct risk analyses and monitor and control trade flows. SINDA was designed with several objectives in mind: to meet the WCO requirements, to simplify and expedite customs clearance procedures, and to ensure that customs laws and regulations were enforced.[9]

Besides SINDA, and with the same objective of reducing corruption, Tunisia established a "single report" system (*système de liasse unique*) in 2007. This established an information technology (IT) connection between the Tunisian Port Authority and customs services and maritime agents. The seaport of Radès is the only port that currently applies the automation system. Single reporting makes it possible to standardize documentation and creates an integrated platform for automated data analysis.

This reform came on the heels of the single window for external trade, which the Higher Council of Exports created in 2002. However, the real impetus for automation had come from the creation in 2000 of Tunisie TradeNet. This network manages the connections between the data in the "single report system" and the users. Service users can connect to the network, through either an information exchange system or the Internet, after signing an agreement with the General Directorate for Customs. Tunisie TradeNet has played a prominent role in reducing paperwork and simplifying procedures over the past decade. It has made possible the use of other IT-enabled reforms, including electronic external trade certificates in 2004, electronic signatures in 2006, and the transmission of entry summary declarations in 2010.

Finally, in line with the customs-to-customs partnership goal promoted by the WCO, *ex post* controls were established to create an efficient risk management system. These controls are carried out after the customs release note is issued, regardless of the type of control (physical, documentation, investigation, and so forth).

All these reforms have helped give Tunisia a good reputation for having successfully reformed its customs service in line with the recommendations of the WCO[10] and international donors. The reforms were reflected in global indicators and became part of the Tunisian "economic miracle" storyline. According to the *Logistics Performance Index*, Tunisia ranked higher than any other country in the Middle East and North Africa, scoring 2.84 out of a possible 5. By comparison, the Arab Republic of Egypt scored 2.61, Morocco 2.38, and Algeria 2.36. According to *Doing Business 2013*, Tunisia also performed better than other countries in the region for cross-border trade. The country ranked 31 globally, ahead of Morocco (37), leaving Turkey (86), Egypt (83), and Algeria (133) far behind.[11]

Nevertheless, and despite the bullish global rankings, experts of the Tunisian customs have continued to depict a less rosy reality that is rife with discrepancies between reforms on paper and their actual implementation. The next section takes a closer look at this enforcement gap and its possible causes.

Partial and Discretionary Enforcement of Customs Rules

The previous section showed that Tunisia introduced procedures to facilitate trade through the simplification of customs clearance procedures and promote integrity through automation.[12] This section provides evidence of the selective and discretionary implementation of some reforms and lack of implementation altogether of others.

On paper, automation should have curtailed customs agents' face-to-face contact with brokers. In practice, printed declarations and supporting documents still need to be presented to a customs official in person. In consequence, the benefits of automation have not been realized, physical interaction is still required, and the risk of corruption persists. On top of this, according to the Union Tunisienne de l'Industrie, du Commerce et de l'Artisanat (2013), certified customs brokers only handle one declaration in five. Part-time unlicensed brokers handle most declarations in public areas that the customs service makes available. Consequently, unfair competition exists between brokers who pay a fee for access to Tunisie TradeNet and those who do not. This results in poorly enforced regulations, weaker controls, and a security risk because part-time unlicensed brokers lack experience and may wish to collude with customs officials to avoid being examined.

As in most countries, the selection of the customs channel (green, orange, or red) is based on objective criteria: scoring, exception regimes, and random assignments. However, Tunisia has many more rules governing exceptions than other countries. The Tunisian customs authorities have (mis)used the exception regime (green or red), which is normally based on the type, country of origin, and value of the goods, to fully exempt specific importers, such as some foreign embassies and politically connected businesses, from any controls while subjecting others to full physical inspection regardless of the nature, country of origin, and value of the goods.

The room to exercise such discretion was built into the risk analysis system for channel selection. It makes it possible to unfairly favor one company over others by systematically assigning its competitors' freight to the red channel. Furthermore, exceptions can be made at the request of the government—for example, the Ministry of Finance or the Ministry of Industry—raising concerns about collusive practices.

Over the past five years, 80 percent of declarations assigned to the red channel did not bring in additional revenues, indicating a misuse of the red channel for reasons other than detecting fraud. That inspectors do not generate additional revenues when they trigger physical inspections means the likelihood of them striking unofficial bargains is relatively high. Also, the rules relating to selectivity and targeting are inappropriate and inefficient. Presently only customs staff from the IT department can modify selectivity criteria. This lack of oversight from customs agents creates concerns that the system is unreliable.

Anecdotal evidence points to occasional manipulation of selectivity criteria by way of setting unit prices according to the identity of importers.[13] At the same time, the risk analysis appears to be too narrow because it does not take into consideration the intervention of a customs official. At most, the analysis results in goods being assigned to another customs channel. A reform to address these issues has been considered but not yet implemented.

Also, the numerous duty suspension regimes may well have made the Authorized Economic Operator status less attractive, with only nine companies having requested this status for a long time. The requirements to benefit from these suspension regimes are so minimal that most importers meet them. These duty suspension regimes offer the same advantages as the Authorized Economic Operator label without necessarily facing the same constraints. Their sheer number also makes the discretionary enforcement of rules more likely and opens the door to corruption.

Preventive measures such as simplified procedures and tariffs are not enough on their own to solve the complex problem of corruption in revenue collection (Casanegra de Jantscher and Bird 1992; Chambas 1994).[14] The larger, systemic problem confronting Tunisia is the failure to enforce these rules. It could result from political interference, and certainly points toward collusion between customs officials and importing firms. Ayadi, Raballand, and de Rochambeau (2015) used statistical analyses, interviews, and survey data to illustrate pervasive fraud resulting from the lack of systematic enforcement of duty suspension regimes. They demonstrated that systematic undervaluation of goods in some bonded warehouses (*magasins et aires de dédouanement*—MAD) led to revenue losses estimated at more than US$150 million a year.

Moreover, for a "partially exporting" firm to buy the inputs without paying value-added tax, it must obtain authorization from the director general of customs. This complex, costly, and lengthy procedure also invites collusion. The nature of the relationship between the manager of the firm and the director general of customs often shapes the outcome. For instance, some firms have access to "ready-made authorizations" by way of pre-stamped notebooks, while other firms do not. In this way, goods can be imported even as they are prohibited, and they can remain on the Tunisian market for many years after. Tracking these goods is difficult, so taxes on them can be easily evaded. The possibility of establishing "fictive warehouses," as per Articles 141–144 of the Tunisian customs code, compounds the problem.

With the approval of the customs service (under Article 142), any trading firm can establish a fictive warehouse anywhere in the country for up to two years, whenever "the needs of the economy require it." This requires a permanent customs control and that a customs agent is assigned to a warehouse. Yet the large number of warehouses in the country—over 4,000, and many of them fictive—makes it impossible for customs officials to monitor them all.

Furthermore, scanning technology, a potentially efficient tool, appears to be used either too much or too little. The Tunisian customs service installed two fixed and two mobile scanners in Radès, and connected them to SINDA. They adopted a policy of systematic, 100 percent scanning after the release of the goods. Therefore, in principle, all containers and trailer trucks are inspected by scanner, despite having already been physically inspected. Even more, goods are scanned *after* issuing of good to release notes. One third of customs agents in the Radès port, about 80 out of 240 staff, are assigned to the scanner unit, which entails high personnel costs.

Scanning appears to be used as an additional bureaucratic step in customs clearance, instead of a complementary time and personnel-saving tool that enables the customs service to better fit the situation. Anecdotal evidence suggests that scanning has not resolved the problems of discretionary implementation of procedures and differential treatment of operators. It also does not seem to have been particularly successful in detecting fraud: despite a 100 percent scanning policy, official figures only record around 300 cases of fraud (including many cases of illegal migrants in containers), out of nearly 350,000 boxes scanned every year, a ratio of less than 0.1 percent.

This means that the current policy of systematic scanning is not being enforced, putting some importers above the law, or that detected cases of fraud are not recorded. In either case, the policy of systematic as opposed to risk-based scanning is likely to lead to increased rent-extraction.

Furthermore, *ex post* controls appear to be too limited in scope, despite the recent reforms to strengthen them. No formal procedure for *ex post* control is yet in place, nor is an effective overall structure in place. One such control measure, the "back page of the customs declaration" (*verso de déclaration*), which allows customs agents to record their observations, is clearly underused, if used at all. Audits of select monitored economic operators and sectors following the completion of customs declarations are needed to verify their accuracy.

By the same token, apart from the Temporary Admission regimes, no links exist between entry summary declarations and good to release notes. Finally, SINDA appears to suffer serious shortcomings of automation and transparency.

First, and despite automation, continued reliance on manual procedures remains a source for concern. In the case of the transit regime, for example, the only proof that goods left Tunisian territory is a single hand-punched stamp on the transit declaration. Similarly, because the exit form is still filled manually, efforts to expedite procedures have not been as successful as they might otherwise have been. In such instances, contacts between customs officials and importers are inevitable, and with greater interaction, the risk of striking deals "under the table" increases.

At the same time, the use of manual procedures documents makes it impossible to obtain a valid time stamp since the data can be easily tampered with. Measuring the length of the customs clearance process with any accuracy becomes virtually impossible. Second, only the latest iteration of a customs document is retained in SINDA, and when a customs declaration is amended, the original is cancelled before a new one can be issued.

Third, the electronic payment process is not efficient because it is impossible to use the "e-dinar card" to make payments larger than TD1,000. Relatedly, the absence of any automated exchange of information between SINDA and the Public Treasury increases the risk of fraud and mistakes, because information from the customs service has to be inputted manually into the Treasury's database.

Sources of the Implementation Gap

Human Resources Management, Performance Monitoring, and Internal Incentives

The number of customs service employees increased significantly between 1995 and 2008. Tunisian customs had 6,200 staff in 2011, 50 percent more than neighboring Morocco's 4,450 in 2013, despite Morocco having a population three times as large and longer land borders (table 4.1).

The number of customs service employees increased significantly between 1995 and 2008.[15] Tunisian customs had 6,200 staff in 2011, 50 percent more than neighboring Morocco's 4,450 in 2013, despite Morocco having a population three times as large and longer land borders (table 4.1).[16]

Recently, there has also been a high turnover among senior managers, with five heads of customs appointed in just two years. This overstaffing is reflected in the wage bill and means that the cost of enforcing customs laws and regulations has consistently exceeded customs revenues since 2001 (figure 4.2).

Besides its bloated workforce, the Tunisian customs service suffers internal accountability issues. It is currently not possible to monitor customs officials' actions using either SINDA or other procedures as currently followed. Staff incentives and penalties are also inefficient and poorly designed.[17] Customs

Table 4.1 Comparison of Staffing/Population and Kilometers of Land Borders

Country	Number of staff per million inhabitants	Number of staff per kilometer of land border
Tunisia	574	4
Morocco	136	2

Figure 4.2 Costs of Customs Administration since 2001

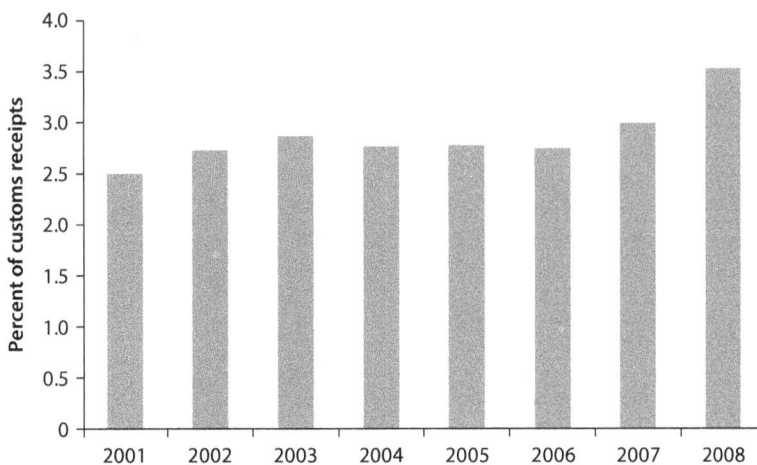

Source: Tunisian Customs.

agents in management positions have not received bonuses since 1981, and some managers may actually earn less than their subordinates (see table 4.2). As a result, customs officials are disinclined to take up management positions, preferring positions elsewhere in the service, such as in operations. Moreover, recruitment and promotions rely mainly on discretionary criteria, resulting in different treatment of employees within the same organization.

Staff penalties are not based on any established criteria and are not codified.[18] Incentives are insufficient to discourage fraud. An agent who uncovers fraud is entitled to TD20 per customs declaration, not a percentage of the value of the goods.[19] The temptation to accept bribes is strong, especially when dealing with high-value imports. A change of policy was considered, but was never taken forward. As an example, duties owed on a container of televisions would be approximately TD7,500. If the importer offered a customs agent only 5 percent of this amount, the agent would stand to earn TD375, 20 times more than he would be formally entitled to and almost as much as his monthly salary.

Favoritism is reportedly rampant, especially in connection with recruitment, promotions, postings, and transfers. Candidates for positions with the customs service are often hired based on favoritism rather than qualifications or skills. Most customs officials remain in their positions for three to four years before being transferred. Officers are given little notice of any change in their position or location, and they have no say in the matter. Because there are no performance reviews, new postings and transfers are usually not based on merit (MCC 2014), and custom officers suffer from low morale because they are deprived of the opportunity to be evaluated fairly.

Lack of Capacity or a Deliberate Failure to Enforce Rules Evenly?

Shortcomings in a customs service are typically blamed on a lack of capacity. This may well be true, but as was argued in chapter 1, there are reasons to suspect that weak capacity in the Tunisians customs service is intentional, at least to some degree. Several examples support such a conclusion. For instance, several years ago, an attempt was made to set individual performance standards for customs

Table 4.2 Wages per Selected Grades and Functions in Customs (in TD)

Grade and function	Wages for management positions (no overtime paid)	Wages for other positions (overtime paid)	Difference between management salaries and others in same grade
Colonel/Director	586.8	629.3	−42.5
Colonel/Vice Director	576.8	629.3	−52.5
Colonel, Department	576.8	629.3	−52.5
Major	498.4	495	+3.4
Major/C.S.	452.5	495	−42.5
Captain	471	438.5	+33.4
Captain/C.S.	426	438.5	−12.5

Source: Tunisian Customs, 2013 data.
Note: C.S. = Chef de Service, TD = Tunisian dinar.

agents with the objective of promoting accountability. This never got off the ground, however, and no such standards exist today. Another example concerns decisions about where to deploy staff. For example, the number of inspectors responsible for physically monitoring cargo in Radès is far lower than the number of customs officials in charge of the more trivial responsibility of scanning goods.

Similarly troubling, less than 1 percent of Tunisian customs officials are responsible for *ex post* controls. Agents generally prefer to work in central administrative units where they are better paid and enjoy more benefits, and the customs service human resources do not do anything to discourage this trend.[20] Without strong *ex post* controls, the duty suspension regimes could potentially lower revenue collection and increase corruption among customs officials. The fear of losing the possibility to give and accept bribes in exchange for favorable treatment in customs is likely to be the reason why, despite many donor recommendations, *ex post* controls are not welcomed by some customs officials and importers.

Rijkers, Baghdadi, and Raballand (2015) present evidence suggesting that firms owned by former President Ben Ali and his family were more likely to evade import tariffs. During Ben Ali's reign, evasion gaps[21] were correlated with the import share of connected firms. This association appears especially strong in those goods subject to high tariffs. It is driven by underreporting of unit prices, which diminished after the revolution. Therefore, customs favoritism was most probably instrumental in helping Ben Ali firms make more profit than competitors.

Finally, according to Beatrice Hibou (2011), the dichotomy between exporting and nonexporting firms is likely to have been created in the Ben Ali era to create a favorable impression of Tunisia's economic performance abroad despite the inequalities and distortions it created. Hibou explains: "Once [foreign firms] have passed the entrance gate into Tunisia, they are protected from the predatory activities of greedy intermediates. Since most [foreign] firms were investing in sectors that had been considered to be high priority by the central power, the latter would do everything to abide by the rules and even distort or violate some of these rules to the advantage of foreigners." Hibou then goes on to describe how foreign companies were generally exempted from several predatory practices and were "fast tracked" during Ben Ali's time.

The Eroding Efficiency of Customs

Absent additional data, and given the type of information this study relied on— mainly anonymous interviews with senior officials of the Tunisian customs service and other close observers—it is not possible to draw a direct causal link between the discretionary enforcement of good rules and the eroding efficiency of the Tunisians customs service in recent years. Yet such evidence of efficiency losses is increasingly obvious.

Three indicators are typically used to assess the performance of the customs service in developing countries: revenue generation, for instance as a percentage of gross domestic product (GDP) or of the value of imports; processing time, whether the time needed to process customs declarations or cargo "dwell" time;

and the control of corruption and fraud. On the first performance indicator, revenue collection, customs agents have been recovering less and less in custom duties since 2001, relative to GDP and compared to Morocco, a neighboring country at a similar level of development. Indeed, the Moroccan customs service collects nearly double the revenues as Tunisia despite having a lower average applied tariff rate (15.5 percent in Morocco; more than 20 percent in Tunisia). The ratio of customs revenues to GDP in Tunisia fell to 5.7 percent in 2010 from 6.7 percent in 2001 (figure 4.3), whereas in Morocco it increased to 9.6 percent in 2010 from 8.8 percent in 2004.

On the second indicator, processing times, extremely low turnarounds of less than a day in 2010, may lead one to believe that Tunisia is a particularly high performer. A closer look reveals that this indicator is misleading at best, because it relies on a narrow definition of customs activity, such as the time taken to process a customs declaration form after it has been electronically recorded. From the perspective of the importer, however, what really matters is the time it takes for freight to leave the port after it has arrived. In Tunisia, it takes over 6 days on average before freight leaves the port,[22] and almost 10 days for consumption goods, according to the World Bank's assessment of the investment climate.[23] In the fight against fraud, Tunisian customs collected TD26 million in fines, representing 1 percent of total revenue in 2012. Earlier figures are not available. Nevertheless, in post-revolution Tunisia, the customs service has been accused of corruption and criticized for having been too accommodating to the former regime.[24] Further research is needed to make the causal link between discretionary implementation of relatively good rules as described above and efficiency losses in Tunisian customs, but the correlation trends are visible.

One conclusion of this chapter is that less emphasis ought to be given to legal reforms, such as the revision of the customs code, and to improving capacity, such

Figure 4.3 Trends in Customs Revenues in Morocco and Tunisia (Percent of GDP)

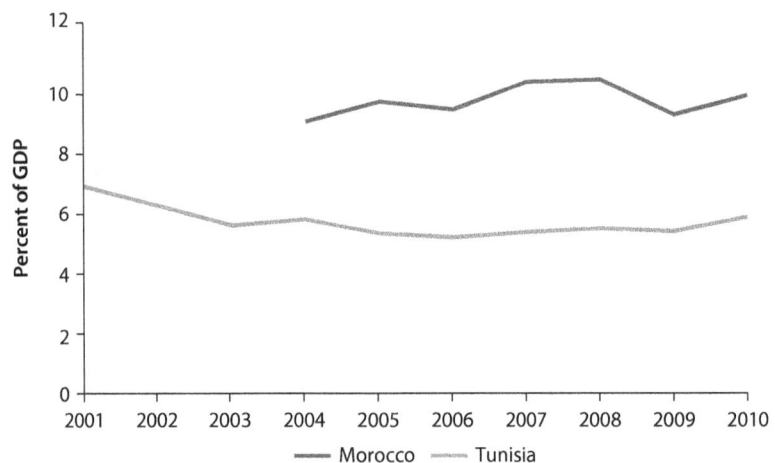

Source: Tunisia and Morocco Customs.

as the adoption of more sophisticated information technology, and more attention should be paid to improving individual and organizational incentives, such as those provided in human resources policies. A related observation is that most challenges faced by the Tunisian customs service result from the discretionary and selective enforcement of rules, which undermines efficiency and leaves the door open for collusive practices.

Political interference and rents redistribution in an opaque and complex environment make discretionary enforcement possible (Hibou 2011). In Tunisia, customs rules on paper are by and large sound, but "practical norms"—how the rules are implemented, who gains from selective enforcement, and why—appear to matter more than the quality of the rules themselves. Tunisia adopted a revised customs strategy in September 2015. Reform of human resources is a major element of this strategy. Time will tell if this reform will change incentives and behavior.

Notes

1. According to the head of customs, Tunisia was on track to become a signatory of the Kyoto convention in 2014.

2. In Tunisia, many reforms were recommended in the context of the Columbus Program, adopted in 2007. The program is the largest and most comprehensive customs capacity-building initiative launched by the WCO. Among its objectives is the full implementation of WCO conventions and instruments, and the use of best practices in customs administration.

3. The origin of goods is a pivotal notion in customs legislation that was largely influenced by Tunisia's admission to the World Trade Organization. Origin refers to the goods' nation of origin and has two variations: preferential origin and nonpreferential origin. The latter is the common regime and is defined by Article 21 of the customs code. A product is considered to be from a given country when it is produced totally or is substantially transformed in that country (that is, 40 percent of local value added). By comparison, preferential origin is based on bilateral or multilateral agreements and entails advantages and tax breaks for both exports and imports.

4. The new Tunisian customs code forbids all imports, exports, and transit of counterfeit goods throughout Tunisian territory, and empowers customs agents to seize counterfeit goods.

5. Geourjon and Laporte (2004) showed that by using a scoring mechanism, physical controls could be relaxed without risk of losing customs revenues.

6. A company is considered "fully exporting" if: (a) the goods and services it produces are exported in their entirety (Articles 10–13 of Tunisia's investment code); (b) it deals with a firm located in a business park (law 2001-76) or (c) a nonresident credit institution; that is, exclusively for nonresidents (law 2009-64).

7. Since January 2012, "fully exporting firms" have had to pay an export tax of 10 percent.

8. An Authorized Economic Operator is a party involved in the international movement of goods in whatever function has been approved by or on behalf of a national customs administration as complying with WCO or equivalent supply-chain security standards. Authorized Economic Operators include, inter alia, manufacturers, importers, exporters, brokers, and so on.

9. Although the system has resulted in noticeable progress in reducing paperwork, it has been necessary to upgrade SINDA repeatedly to meet the customs service's needs. In 2001, the former system migrated to a new platform called SINDA 2000. Since 2010, every operator's fiscal identification (provided by the tax service) is now automatically integrated into the system.

10. For a list and details on the main legal instruments related to WCO areas of intervention, see www.wcoomd.org/en/about-us/legal-instruments.aspx.

11. See http://www.doingbusiness.org/data/exploretopics/trading-across-borders for more information.

12. While many of the rules and policies governing the Tunisian Customs Service were good practice rules, some clearly were not. An example is Tunisia's average applied tariff rate. Even with preferences factored in, the average tariff remains high in comparison to other MENA countries, including Morocco. The rate is 21.5 percent in Tunisia as opposed to 16.8 percent in Algeria, 15.5 percent in Morocco, and 10.7 percent in Egypt. A rate so high could potentially hinder formal trade.

13. For instance, the system is designed in such a way that if declared values are too low—thereby indicating undervaluation of the value of the goods—an alert is triggered signaling likely fraud. However, if manipulation takes place and the alert level is set at an exaggeratedly low value to favor a particular importer (say at 10 instead of 50 for other importers), this importer's goods will not trigger the alert system and fraud will go undetected.

14. These authors suggest some ways that the fiscal collection system could be improved for greater efficiency and accountability.

15. The number of officials at certain ranks has increased threefold in recent years.

16. Tunisia shares 1,424 kilometers of land borders and Morocco 2,018 kilometers (CIA, The World Factbook database).

17. Since the Jasmine Revolution not a single employee has been sanctioned for corruption.

18. This is especially problematic at borders (with Libya for instance) where informal trade seems to have grown significantly and customs staff practices seem to contradict the customs code (Ayadi et al. 2013).

19. In case of a fraud uncovered, 20 percent of the value of the goods is credited to a customs collective fund while 60 percent accrues to the Treasury.

20. For instance, health and transport services are supposed to be free for all customs officials. Because they are offered only in Tunis, however, only officials working for the central administration can benefit.

21. Evasion gaps are defined as the difference between the value of exports to Tunisia as reported by trade partners and the value of imports as reported at the Tunisian customs.

22. This is for the clearance of imported goods. For exporters of manufactured goods importing on duty suspension schemes, customs clearance times are lower.

23. Anecdotal evidence suggests customs agents have manipulated data. Knowing that the clock starts ticking when the declaration is entered into the computer system, and that it stops when a release certificate is issued, customs officials might come to an agreement with brokers to record the declaration at the last minute, after having "negotiated" the terms of the declaration "under the table." It is also possible that customs officials issue a release certificate and then modify the customs declaration.

24. Delavallade (2012), based on surveys of businesses in North Africa. The author draws a connection between corruption and tax evasion, one of the most common forms of corruption in the private sector.

References

Ayadi, L., N. Benjamin, S. Bensassi, and G. Raballand. 2013. "Estimating Informal Trade Across Tunisia's Land Borders." World Bank Policy Research Working Paper 6731, World Bank, Washington, DC.

Ayadi, L., G. Raballand, and G. de Rochambeau. 2015. "Fraud Risks in Customs Bonded Warehouses in Tunisia." *Global Trade and Customs Journal.* 10 (11–12): 417–25.

Casanegra de Jantscher, M., and R. Bird. 1992. "The Reform of Tax Administration." In *Improving Tax Administration in Developing Countries,* edited by M. Casanegra de Jantscher and R. Bird. Washington, DC: International Monetary Fund.

Chambas, G. 1994. *Fiscalité et Développement en Afrique sub-saharienne.* Paris: Economica.

De Herdt, Tom, and Jean-Pierre Olivier de Sardan. 2015. *Real Governance and Practical Norms in Sub-Saharan Africa.* London: Routledge.

Delavallade, C. 2012. "What Drives Corruption? Evidence from North African Firms." *Journal of African Economies* 21 (4): 499–547.

Geourjon, A.-M., and B. Laporte. 2004. "Risk Management for Targeting Customs Controls in Developing Countries: A Risky Venture for Revenue Performance?" *Study and Documents,* CERDI (Centre d'Études et de Recherches sur le Développement International).

Hibou, Béatrice. 2011. *The Force of Obedience.* Cambridge, UK: Polity.

MCC (Millennium Challenge Corporation). 2014. *Tunisia Threshold Program Sector Analysis and Program Design.* Report on Governance. Millennium Challenge Corporation, Washington, DC.

Mishra, P., A. Subramanian, and P. Topalova. 2008. "Policies, Enforcement, and Customs Evasion: Evidence from India." *Journal of Public Economics* 92: 1907–25.

Rijkers, Bob, Leila Baghdadi, and Gaël Raballand. 2015. "Political Connections and Tariff Evasion: Evidence from Tunisia." World Bank Policy Research Working Paper 7336, World Bank, Washington, DC.

Union Tunisienne de l'Industrie, du Commerce et de l'Artisanat. 2013. "Les Professions Maritimes en Crise." Presented on April 26, 2013, Tunis.

CHAPTER 5

Exclusion and Norms: Enforcing Women's Rights to Property in Jordan

Property ownership is a male domain in Jordan, where women are dependent on men for housing. A patriarchal pattern of power dominates both inheritance and property. While the inheritance rights of women are formally enshrined in the constitution, in Islamic law (Sharia), and in the customary law particularly common in the steppe regions, female heirs continue to face social pressure to renounce their rights in favor of male heirs. Most women either do not receive the share of inheritance that the law entitles them to or they are simply denied their right to housing and land.

Jordanian Sharia Court data show that in 2014 a third of heirs fully relinquished their inheritance rights through the process of *takhāruj*, the voluntary "opting out" of their rights (exclusion). Records do not specify their gender, but survey evidence shows most of those who requested *takhāruj* were women. A survey conducted in the Irbid governorate in 2010 by the Jordanian National Forum for Women indicated that 20 percent of women had renounced their inheritance rights and that three-quarters of them had done so willingly. Jordanian women still appear to abide by the belief that they will harm the economic and social status of their brothers if they take up their right to inheritance. These social norms and beliefs have led Jordanian women to internalize and condone the privileges of men in matters of inheritance.

Besides social pressure, women are deprived of their inheritance in several other ways. One takes the form of a donation to male heirs before a person's death. Another is when owners and their male heirs choose to leave a property undivided, which prevents female heirs from using or selling their share for years and even decades. This often happens with agricultural land and family-owned buildings. In most cases male heirs give symbolic gifts to women, called *badal* or *takrīm*, which are worth far less than the value of shares they are legally entitled to receive. In general, women are kept in the dark about the real value of assets such as land or an apartment.

As a consequence of such cultural norms, only 6.8 percent of ever married women owned their houses and only 7 percent owned land in 2012 (Jordanian Department of Statistics [DOS and ICF 2013]). A recent trend has seen women managing to register residential apartments in their name upon marriage, mainly in the major cities of Amman and Irbid. Women owned 19.5 percent of registered apartments in Jordan in 2014 (HKJ 2014). But since apartments constitute 42 percent of housing units, mainly built as a form of investment, that translates into women owning a mere 10 percent of all apartments. In comparison, women owned 22.5 percent of securities, whether bonds, shares, or options in 2011 (DOS and KVINFO 2012). Husbands often register apartments and securities in the name of their wives to protect their assets from creditors, if their business goes bankrupt.

Less than 3 percent of Jordanian people are Christian, but historically they have owned large tracts of land and are significant players in the nation. Sharia law has been applied to Christian property inheritance since the Ottoman period in Jordan, and although Christian tradition stipulates that women be granted the same shares as men, Christian deputies have never asked for the inheritance law to be revised.

Women's rights activists have succeeded in amending the Jordanian Personal Status Law No. 36 of 2010 by working with the Sharia Supreme Court (Qādī al-Qudā), the country's highest religious and legal institution. In 2011 seven amendments were made and two articles added: articles 318 and 319 on property and exclusion. The most important amendment introduced a mandatory three months after the death of the owner before either exclusion (*takhāruj*) or power of attorney (*wakāla*) could be invoked. Another amendment stated that an attorney dealing with an estate was under obligation to inform the heirs of all properties included in an inheritance. Another specified that a judge must explain to the heirs the legal consequences of the exclusion of inheritance; this has resulted in judges asking for better education for women so that they can better defend their rights.

The improvement of women's rights to inheritance has been proffered since the 1960s as a solution to poverty and a means of preventing women from falling into destitution. Property rights and security of tenure are basic not only to shelter but also to improvement of livelihoods, economic prosperity, and sustainable development.[1] The United Nations' human settlement program, UN-Habitat, and the Office of the High Commissioner for Human Rights support property rights and the security of tenure under the Right to Adequate Housing Framework. Jordan is working on incentives for better inclusion of women in the economy, and inheritance and property should be a major dimension of this policy.

This chapter applies the conceptual framework for the enforcement of the rule of law to housing and property rights in Jordan, focusing on voluntary and forced exclusions of women from property ownership. The main argument is that the gender inequality embedded in the inheritance system creates a "glass ceiling" that hinders the economic and social progress of women in Jordan.

Inheritance is one of three pillars of economic independence for women, with dowry and employment. However, in Jordan, these pillars do not stand on solid foundations. A 2010 World Economic Forum report on gender gaps ranks Jordan 120th among 134 countries in women's economic opportunities, well below many other middle-income countries (World Bank 2013a).

Fieldwork for this chapter was conducted in two areas of East Amman, Wadi Abdoun and Jabal Nuzha, in September and October 2015. Interviews with judges of the Sharia Supreme Court, lawyers from women's rights organizations, and lawyers and engineers from the Department of Land and Survey (DLS) and the Housing and the Urban Development Corporation were conducted in October and November of the same year.

The first section of the chapter presents findings on the economic and social context of housing and land fragmentation in Jordan. The second focuses on the evolution of the legal framework governing inheritance and land property in Jordan. The third examines pressures on women to waive their inheritance rights. The final section looks at advocacy work carried out by women's rights organizations guided by the United Nations' Convention on the Elimination of All Forms of Discrimination Against Women (CEDAW).

Women's Islamic Rights to Inheritance

Since the Ottoman Empire (1516–1918), inheritance procedures have been governed by Sharia (Islamic) principles embedded in the customary law of *Liwa 'Ajlun*, the heart of the region that became the Emirate of Transjordan in 1921. In 1869, these rules were codified by the Ottoman Family of Law (*Al Majelle*). Inheritance, marriage, and divorce today are all governed by personal law on the basis of Islamic principles for Muslims citizens. Jordanian Christians, who share a common culture with Muslims about the importance of acquiring and transferring land, have applied Sharia law to matters of inheritance in their own courts and tribunals for decades.

The Legal Framework for Inheritance

In Jordan the rights of men and women to inheritance are guaranteed by civil law and the personal affairs law. Both are based on the 1869 law that applies Islamic Sharia principles. According to this law, women receive half of their brother's share, but more of their husband's estate: a quarter if the widow had no children and an eighth if she had children. This was decided by the Jordanian Civil Law (Article 1086) and is stated in the last amendment of the Provisional Jordanian Personal Status Law, number 36 of 2010 (see box 5.1).

Non-Muslims are not permitted to inherit from Muslims, which is a reason for some women to convert to Islam. Under Sharia, inheritance cannot pass to a murderer, nor can it go to an individual who has given false testimony that resulted in someone's execution (Jordanian National Forum for Women 2012).

Rules on Paper, Rules in Practice • http://dx.doi.org/10.1596/978-1-4648-0886-9

Box 5.1 Inheritance Divisions According to the Qur'an (Sunni Tradition)

Children's shares:
- If several male and female children survive the deceased, the inheritance is divided according to the rule that a male heir receives twice as much as a female heir.
- If, along with children, the deceased has spouse(s) or parents, they inherit first (according to the proportions stated below). The children receive the rest, with male heirs getting twice as much as females.
- An only child who is male receives the whole inheritable estate. An only child who is female receives half of the inheritable estate.

Parents' shares:
- If the deceased is survived by children, the mother and father of the deceased both receive one-sixth of the estate.
- If the deceased leaves no children, the mother receives one-third and the father two-thirds.
- If the deceased has two or more siblings, the mother receives one-sixth, the father five-sixths, and the siblings are not entitled to anything.

The husband's share:
- If the wife dies and leaves no children, the husband receives half of the estate.
- If the wife dies and is survived by children, the husband receives one-quarter.

The share/shares of the wife/wives
- Note that when more than one wife survives the husband, each wife is entitled to receive an equal share of the following allotments:
- If the husband dies and leaves no children, the wife or wives are entitled to receive one-quarter of the estate.
- If the husband dies and does leave children, the share going to the wife/wives is one-eighth of the estate.

Shares of uterine brothers/sisters:
- If the deceased has one sibling from the same mother, the sibling receives one-sixth of the estate.
- If the deceased has two or more siblings from the same mother, they together receive one-third.

Shares of full or agnatic brothers/sisters:
- If the deceased has brothers/sisters from the same two parents or only the same father, the inheritance is divided according to the rule that brothers receive twice as much as sisters.
- In most cases, the widow receives one-eighth of the estate, the parents of the deceased receive one-sixth each, and the children are entitled to what remains, with male heirs getting twice as much as female heirs.

Source: COHRE 2006, p. 12.

Money and Immovable Properties

Women have full legal personality and as such can handle property and conduct financial deals. This right is given by the Sharia and guaranteed under civil law. An adult woman is not required to have a male guardian over her property and she can buy, sell, lease, mortgage, and grant the power of attorney. The Provisional Jordanian Personal Status Law number 36 of 2010 stipulates in Article 320, "Each of the spouses shall have separate financial liability" (Jordanian National Forum for Women 2012).

Two types of inheritance exist in Jordan: property, which covers land and housing (*amwāl 'aqārāt*), and financial, which covers assets in banks or companies (*amwāl naqdīa*). The Sharia court (mahkamat al-Shari'a) grants a share of financial inheritance to all heirs over the age of 18, including women. Each heir receives a check in their name and the inheritance is taxed at 3 percent by the Sharia court. The heir is not able to be excluded from this. In practice women who receive checks are also required to give this money to their mother or their brothers. However, often, they do not comply with this request.

Before the 1970s, most Jordanian women could acquire their own assets only through inheritance and dowry (Jansen 1993). The 1970s oil boom opened up the job market for women, making it more possible to obtain financial capital independent of husbands. Women from the Christian minority were disproportionately engaged in economic activity; a third of employed women were Christian in 1969[2] (Jansen 1993).

Legal Procedures and Family Negotiations

The very procedure of inheritance is dealt with by men, and women are at best consulted. To receive their legal rights, heirs must obtain a medical report attesting to the death of the deceased and the death certificate (*shahadat wafā*) from the Bureau of Civil Affairs (ahwāl madaniya). The heirs must then obtain a letter (*kitāb li da'irat al-'araḍi*) from the Islamic Tribunal (mahkamat al-Shari'a) requesting the DLS to issue a report on the property (*kashaf al-'amlāk*) to them.[3] Then, the heirs must return to the Islamic tribunal to obtain the proof of inheritance shares (*huja hasr al-irth*). The next step depends on what plans the heirs have for the properties. If the heirs need to sell, then they must go to each of the registration directorates of the DLS (mudiriat tasjīl) in which they own land. Only then can the transfer (*intiqāl*) and division procedures (*ifrāz*) of the estate start. Each heir then obtains a property deed (*sanad tasjīl*) in their own name. The DLS charges a tax of 1 percent of the estimated value of the property.

In most cases after the death of a father, the heirs gather to decide how the property should be divided before going to the court. Instead of dividing the plot of land fairly according to the Sharia, they can decide to exchange, sell, or even renounce their rights. Women rarely attend these family negotiations. If the land is used for farming, no division is made, and the *musha'a* system—in which the earnings from the land are divided between brothers is applied. No legal transaction occurs in such a scenario. This is very common and over the decades has deprived women of their inheritance, as the next section describes.

Once the decision has been agreed, the family has two options. It can choose to have the decision validated in the civil court, in a long process that can take six months to a year and cost thousands of Jordanian dinar (depending on the DLS's estimation of the land value). The other option, which is much more common, is to go to the Sharia court and register the familial decision (*tasjīl al-itifāqīa*), including the various exclusions (*takhāruj*) and powers of attorney (*wakālat*). In most cases, a single male heir will buy the shares of his sisters, in the best case with proper compensation (*badal*).

Most family houses are not registered per se; only the plots of land on which they are built. As a consequence, when a grandfather or father dies, the heirs gather to decide how to use the house, and how to allocate apartments to soon-to-be married children and the father's wife or the widows. This is done through a familial agreement. No legal division of the house takes place. This is especially common for properties located outside municipal zones and serviced-land boundaries. Division usually occurs for properties within municipal boundaries, where land prices have risen significantly in the past 15 years. In cities, houses and apartments are normally sold, and the shares of each heir are defined by the Sharia—with women entitled to specific shares (box 5.1). But most of the time, negotiations are kept in the family to find the best way to give better opportunities to boys by taking part of the daughters' shares, without depriving them too much.

Sharia Is Applied to Muslims and Christians in Matters of Inheritance

Although Christians represent less than 3 percent of Jordan's 9.5 million inhabitants,[4] they have played prominent roles in Jordan's nation-building. The Christian minority bought large tracts of land, especially buys south of Amman by the Aubjaber, Qawar, and Besharat families in the 1850s (Abujaber 1989). A quota of nine seats is reserved for Christian representatives in the Jordanian parliament. Christians are under Hashemite protection, which is a way for the king to place himself in the continuity of Islamic rulers.

In Jordan, the patriarchal hierarchy can be considered as much a marker of the Christian communities as it is of the Muslim communities. The cultural norms of both communities keep wealth in the male line of the family and guard against women disseminating it when marrying. Christians and Muslims have adopted similar strategies to keep control of the land. This is increasingly important in an environment in which land fragmentation is increasingly widespread. As a consequence, Christian communities willingly adhere to the Islamic laws on matters of inheritance.[5] As a judge of the Sharia Supreme Court once remarked, culturally "there is no difference between Christian and Muslim ethnic groups and families in Jordan!" Sharia does in fact protect the rights of Christian girls to a share of inheritance:[6] "Without Sharia law not a single woman would inherit in Jordan," the judge said.[7]

Christians apply the Sharia law to matters of inheritance, as none of the laws of the eleven Christian churches in Jordan concern the distribution of shares. Through the 1989–91 democratic opening of Jordan new laws were adopted in response to the more conservative demands of the Muslim brothers. Among these laws, was the Shifting of Immovable Property Law—Qānūn al-Intiqāl No. 4 1991), according to which the Sharia covers both Muslim and non-Muslim in Jordan. No one contested it, as it served both Muslim and Christians male interests over land and property. Christian officials and prominent Jordanian leaders have not openly discussed the issue of inheritance.[8] Nor has it ever been presented before parliament.

Impact of Land Fragmentation, Urbanization, and Legislation

To better understand the reduced share of women's ownership of housing and land in Jordan, it is important to consider the problem of land fragmentation. This will allow us to better understand the strategies adopted by men to keep control over land and properties.

Customary Law Over Rural and Pastoral Land (mīrī)

Since the Ottoman Empire, and until the 1991 Shifting of Immovable Property Law—Qānūn al-Intiqāl No. 4 1991, two systems of legal rules governed property ownership: the Sharia for private land (mafrūz) and the customary law ('urf) for rural and pastoral land (mīrī). The Ottoman Islamic Land Code of 1858 classified properties into five types: private land (mulk), state-owned land (mīrī), religious endowment (waqf), abandoned land (matruk), and barren land (mawat). Agricultural private and state-owned land were commonly exploited by men, under the musha'a system of collective land use, on a system of rotation. When Transjordan was established, the considerable social control over land was high-lighted by the prevalence of the musha'a exploitation system.[9]

Private property, or mulk, was by definition restricted to urban land (land within the municipal boundaries of villages and towns) and to orchards and olive trees. This private land was governed by the Sharia principles of the Civil Code (Mejelle) introduced in 1869. The best agricultural land was mainly under communal exploitation (musha'a). Farmers and shepherds had rights of use (tasarruf), but the property belonged to the State (mīrī). Customs intervened for mīrī land and, as a consequence, tasarruf rights were inherited equally between men and women (map 5.1).

Land Fragmentation

One of the bases of political stability in Jordan is that, contrary to the Arab Republic of Egypt and the Syrian Arab Republic, the country did not undergo any agrarian reform. Instead, small and medium-size holdings were consolidated by land settlement during the British Mandate, while large landholdings were not affected by land reforms (Fischbach 2000). This enabled prominent tribal and urban families to keep and transform their economic power.

Until the growth of industry in the 1960s, the economy was mostly agrarian and Jordanian society consisted of a minority of influential tribal and urban families and a mass of small-scale farmers. Although the well-known sheikhs and

Map 5.1 Jordan Potential Land Use and Urban Extension

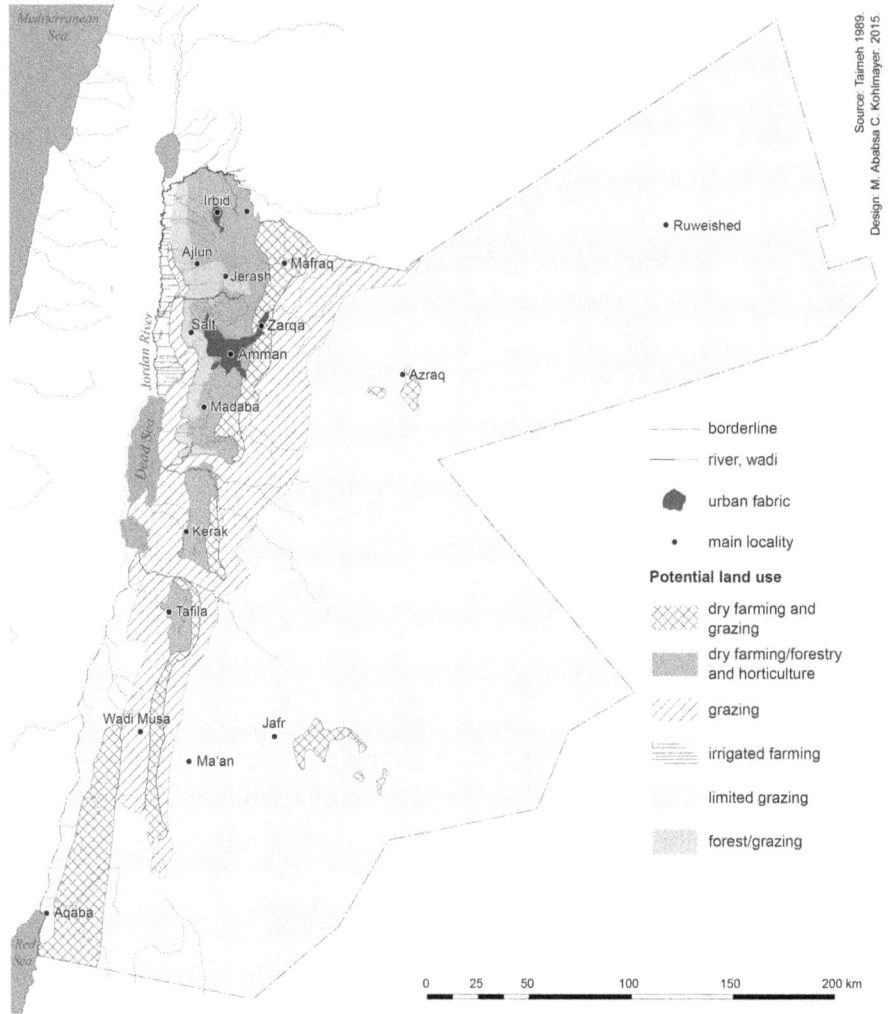

wealthy traders had managed to amass large areas of land, inequality was much lower than in the rest of the *Bilād al-Shām* at this time. Only 17 percent of the land was owned within large estates in 1953, in less than 1 percent of the land holdings (table 5.1).

To increase land productivity, the British introduced major land policy and taxation reform in 1927. One of the aims was to replace the communal system of land ownership with private ownership in an attempt to improve crop yields and expand areas planted with fruit trees. Private ownership was believed to give better yields. However, starting from the 1950s plot size, through inheritance, began to shrink. The old system of *musha'a* keeping land in various forms of collective exploitation had worked over decades to prevent plot fragmentation as only shares of the production were divided. From an average size of 40 donums

Table 5.1   Distribution of Land Holding According to the Size, Jordan, 1953

	%	Area (donums)	%	Number
Small properties < 10 ha	21.3	1,334,652	70.4	40,857
Middle properties 10–100 ha	61.9	3,876,408	28.8	16,718
Large properties > 100 ha	16.8	1,054,045	0.8	451
Total	100	6,265,105	100	58,026

Source: Baer (1957), table 11.

(4 hectares) in the 1920s the average plot size had decreased to 10 donums in the 1950s and farmers had to rent their land (Fischbach 2000).

Land fragmentation continues to be a major issue in Jordan. Small properties of less than 10 ha are forming now 41.6 percent of the cultivated land, while medium size properties were reduced by half (61.9 percent in 1953 to 32.4 percent in 2007).[10] Large estates, went down from 451 to 212, but increased the surface farmed over the same period. To counter further land fragmentation, land owners are preferring not to divide the farmed land and pastoral land at the death of a father or even a grandfather. The elder sons agree about the use of the land, and in most of the cases, the *musha'a* collective system of exploitation is then reintroduced within the members of extended families. By law, the minimum plot size for sale purposes was set at 10 donums until 2001, when it was reduced to 4 donums.[11]

Urban Expansion and Land Speculation

The problem of land fragmentation was partly solved in the cities by modification of the land use, which resulted in rising land values. As a result of the influx of 70,000 Palestinian refugees into Transjordan in 1948—following the establishment of Israel and the rural exodus of farmers whose plots of land were too small to survive on urban growth spiked at the end of the 1940s—the new government of Jordan, assisted by engineers from British Land and Survey, decided to expand municipal boundaries. In 1953 the Law of Converting Land No. 41, which enforced the change of land from *mīrī* to *mulk*, had a positive effect on the price of land within the cities.[12] However, the law harmed women's inheritance rights because it deprived women of equal inheritance rights on former *mīrī* land that was now within municipal boundaries. Women were now entitled to only half the share of their brothers in accordance with Sharia law. "Particularly as towns like Amman expanded into the surrounding farmland, women's inheritance shares in what land they did manage to inherit, shrank" (Fischbach 2000).

Until the 1970s, according to historian Rauf Abujaber, agricultural land was of little value (Abujaber 1989). With the onset of the oil boom and migration of Jordanian engineers to the Gulf, large flows of money started to enter the country. The building of a new airport in 1978 south of Amman had a major influence on the change of land use and economic patterns converting Jordan from an economy based on dry agriculture (wheat and barley) to one using greenhouses to grow vegetables for export to the Gulf markets. From 2000 to 2015, the price of land south of Amman skyrocketed (from Jordanian dinar (JD) 20,000 per donum to JD100,000 and more) while prices in West Amman can be as high as JD500,000 to JD1 million per donum in commercial areas. For most Transjordanians, wealth is linked to land ownership. In a time when inflation is high because of the influx of Iraqi refugees in 2000 and the current Syrian refugee crisis, efforts have been increased to keep property within the family, thereby affecting women's rights to inheritance.

Jordan is a country of landowners. In 2014, 73.1 percent of households owned their house or apartment and less than a quarter rented (23.1 percent). Most of these landowners have added a second or third floor to their properties and have even built houses for their children. This is the case in particular for Jordanians of Transjordanian origin residing in the cities and villages of Irbid, Salt, Ajlun Madaba, Kerak, Ma'an, and Aqaba governorates. This causes problems for tenants who tend to be in the major cities of Amman, Russeifa, and Zarqa, most of whom are of Palestinian origin. In 2013, among low-income families, 44 percent of Jordanians rented (HKJ 2013). In informal areas, developed as extensions of UNRWA Palestinian camps, more than half of the inhabitants have land tenure as they have bought land on which a house was self-built. In East Amman, the price used to be JD1 per square meter in 1967 (Ababsa 2012). As a result, 59.8 percent of East Amman dwellers on informal areas own land.[13]

The Application of Sharia on the Inheritance of Mīrī Land (1991)

Over the 1989–91 democratic opening in Jordan, new laws were adopted in response to the more conservative demands of the Muslim brothers. Among these, under the Shifting of Immovable Property Law—Qānūn al-Intiqāl No. 4 1991, major reform of the inheritance procedure was introduced according to which state (*mīrī*) land would no longer be inherited as it had been for centuries equally between men and women. Advocates of women's rights said they had not noticed this clause among several reforms.

Consequently, all agricultural and pasture land since then is subject to the same Sharia divisions as private land (*mulk*) (table 5.2). This had led to the reduction of women's shares in land in ethnic group areas. The land value increase of former pastoral land that became urbanized east of Amman and east of Zarqa especially can explain this major historical change in the inheritance of state land. Hence the share of the inheritance depends on the date of the death of the deceased. If the deceased passed away before March 16, 1991, women are

Table 5.2 Inheritance of *Mulk* and *Mīrī* Land in Jordan before and after 1991

In Jordan	Before 1991	After 1991 (Qānūn al-Intiqāl No. 4)
Agricultural land (*ard mīrī*)	Rights of use (*tasarruf*) are granted equally to men and women = Customary law ('*urf*)	Sharia law is applied to this land and women start to inherit half of a brother's share
Private property (*ard mulk*)	Sharia inheritance division rules are applied	Sharia inheritance division rules are applied

Table 5.3 Distribution of Property (*mulk, miri*) by Number of Plots and Area

	Number of plots	%	Area (donums)	%
Mulk	2,356,206	76	10,411,622	90
Mīrī	727,797	24	1,193,377	10
Total	3,084,003	100	11,604,999	100

Source: Department of Land and Survey database, prepared on request, 8th December 2015.

supposed to receive the same shares are their brothers and if after that date they receive half.[14]

In December 2015, registered *miri* land represented a quarter of the plots, but only 10 percent of the land owned by Jordanians (table 5.3).

Assessing Women's Ownership of Immovable Property

A wide range of statistics is available for property and housing in Jordan, but it is only recently that gender issues have been taken into consideration. The gender section of the Department of Statistics (DOS) only opened in 2007. The DLS records the gender of the landowners and not that of buyers.[15] The Supreme Sharia Court does not publish data by gender for matters of inheritance exclusion or cases in which the power of attorney is invoked.

The Jordan Population and Family Health Survey 2012 was the first to include a section on women's ownership of assets. Conducted on a representative sample of 15,190 households and 11,352 ever-married women aged 15–49, it gave for the first time a clear picture of women's property in Jordan. In 2012, only 6.8 percent of married women owned their house (3.2 percent alone and 3.5 percent jointly with men), and only 7 percent owned land (3.3 percent alone and 3.5 percent jointly with men), according to DOS and ICF in 2013. Rural women are keener to own land than urban women (9.3 percent versus 6.4 percent). Women who reside in the north of the country, where agricultural land is considered better quality, and in the south, where the ethnic group community is larger, tend to own more land than those in the central region, where, over the years, agricultural land has become increasingly urbanized (near Amman, Russeifa, and Zarqa, for example).

Rural women are less keen to own their house, as they are most of the time hosted in their husband's family building. Of rural women, 4.6 percent own their house (2 percent alone and 2.6 percent jointly) compared to 7.2 percent of urban women (3.5 percent alone and 3.7 percent jointly). However, women who live in the central region, near to the capital, are more likely to own and co-own their house; 7.4 percent versus 6 percent in the north and 4 percent in the south (figure 5.1).

Women with higher education are three times more likely than women with no education to own land (9.3 percent, 4.9 percent alone, 4.1 percent jointly) and a house (10.7 percent to 4.7 percent alone and 5.9 percent jointly). In the highest wealth quintile, women are five times more keen to own land and house

Figure 5.1 Percentage of Ever-Married Women House-Owners, 2012

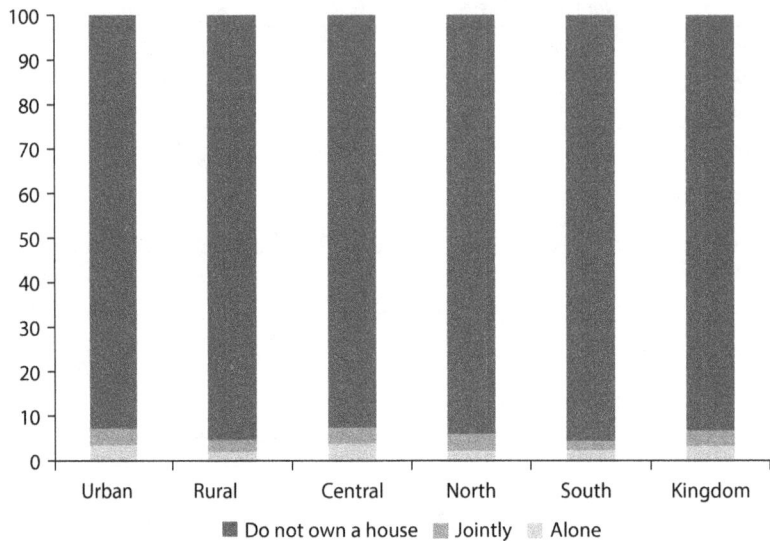

Source: DOS and ICF 2013, JPFHS 2012, table 13.5.

than in the lowest quintile: 13.5 percent of women own land (7.3 percent alone and 6 percent jointly) and 15.3 percent own a house (7.4 percent alone and 7.9 jointly) in the highest quintile, versus 3.1 percent owning land and 2.7 percent owning housing in the lowest quintile (DOS and ICF 2013, JPFHS 2012, table 13.5).

The two governorates where women own the most housing units are Amman and Aqaba (9.2 percent and 8.2 percent). This can be explained by these two governorates absorbing the most foreign direct investments in Jordan. As much money is invested in real estate, men prefer to protect their assets by registering them in the names of their wife and daughters. When the assets are of great value, a power of attorney is signed between husband and wife to stipulate that the wife is not allowed to sell the property without her husband's permission. But in most of the cases, men do not even need this legal proof, as it is well understood that they own the properties registered in their wives' name.

It is important to note that the number of housing units recorded by the census of housing and population is more than double the housing units recorded by the DLS (897,401 against 375,557 in 2014). This is because most houses and buildings have not been divided into separate registered units at the death of their owners. As a result, only 42 percent of apartments (or 375,557) are registered by the cadastre as single units. The rest are included in family buildings and are not registered alone (table 5.4). It is even more difficult for women to inherit unregistered apartments.

On February 4, 2014, 2,965,156 plots of land in private property were registered by the cadastre. Men owned 74.8 percent of these plots, with 20.2 percent owned by women; and 5 percent was registered both men and women (*mushtarak*)

Table 5.4 Difference between DLS-Registered Apartments and the DOS Count

Apartment	Registered by DLS 2014	Total apartment (HEIS 2013)	Unregistered apartment	Unregistered (%)
Amman	253,306	442,126	188,820	42.7
Balqa	9,591	49,268	39,677	80.5
Zarqa	25,572	148,300	122,728	82.8
Madaba	3,692	18,673	14,981	80.2
Irbid	57,652	138,593	80,941	58.4
Mafraq	1,260	11,874	10,614	89.4
Jerash	1,620	19,568	17,948	91.7
Ajlun	2,652	16,373	13,721	83.8
Kerak	5,659	18,377	12,718	69.2
Tafila	1,844	7,258	5,414	74.6
Maan	1,825	6,704	4,879	72.8
Aqaba	10,884	20,127	9,243	45.9
Kingdom	*375,557*	*897,401*	*521,844*	*58.1*

Sources: Department of Land and Survey database prepared on request, November 2015; Department of Statistics. 2015. Household Expenditure and Income Survey 2013, table 1.1.

Table 5.5 Distribution of Land Property in April 2014

LAND	Muchtarak %	Men %	Women %	Total
Irbid	5.8	71.2	23	559,487
Balqa	5	75.3	19.6	151,293
Zarqa	5.1	74.9	20	228,956
Tafila	4.6	78.8	16.6	110,489
Amman	5.2	74.7	20.1	799,238
Aqaba	4.2	77.3	18.5	31,007
Kerak	4.3	78.2	17.5	300,005
Mafraq	4	76.8	19.3	274,543
Jerash	6.1	72.7	21.3	89,110
Ajlun	5.5	69.2	25.4	131,852
Madaba	5.2	74.9	19.9	106,617
Maan	3.9	79.6	16.5	182,559
Kingdom	*5*	*74.8*	*20.2*	*2,965,156*

Source: Department of Land and Survey database prepared by the IT team on request, November 2015.

as owners can have multiple plots[16] (table 5.5). However, one must keep in mind that no data are provided regarding the area of the plots owned by women. The *mushtarak* category includes in most of the case several persons, brothers and sisters, much more that husbands and wives.

On February 4, 2014, Jordanian women owned 24.7 percent of registered apartments (or 92,760), men owned 70 percent (262,889), and the rest was co-owned by men and women (5.3 percent). But the 92,760 registered apartments owned by women represent only 10.3 percent of apartments in Jordan (table 5.6). Since few women in Jordan own unregistered land and houses, the actual

Table 5.6 Distribution of Registered Apartment in April 2014

APARTMENT	Muchtarak %	Men %	Women %	Total
Irbid	5.3	70.7	24.1	57,652
Balqa	4.6	75.1	20.3	9,591
Zarqa	4.7	70.4	24.9	25,572
Tafila	2.4	82.5	15.1	1,844
Amman	5.5	69.1	25.4	253,306
Aqaba	4.1	72.9	23.1	10,884
Kerak	5.1	74.2	20.7	5,659
Mafraq	2.3	76.3	21.3	1,260
Jerash	6.4	72.3	21.3	1,620
Ajlun	4.1	75.7	20.2	2,652
Madaba	4.6	75.4	20	3,692
Maan	2.8	80.2	17	1,825
Kingdom	5.3	70	24.7	375,557

Source: Department of Land and Survey database prepared on request, November 2015.

percentage of immovable properties owned by women is likely more to be about 10 percent of housing units in Jordan, and not the 20 percent always officially stated.

Co-owning property is a solution to protect women's rights to housing, as they would keep half of the apartment at their husband death. In most cases, this shared property recognizes a woman's contribution to the cost of the purchase, through loans. But the number of cases is very low, at 5.3 percent of registered apartments.

The economic damage inflicted on women in inheritance spills over to other domains of economic empowerment, such as acceding to loans. In Jordan, most microloan borrowers are women (76.4 percent of total loans outstanding), although only 15 percent of them work in the formal sector, and only 21.6 percent work in the informal sector. But they signed contracts for only 44.1 percent of total loans by value in 2013.[17] The explanation of this great difference is given by defenders of women's rights: women are encouraged by their husbands to take loans that they will not benefit from directly. This is why two women out of three who apply for loans are not working, either in the formal or in the informal sector.

Property Transfers to Men, Delay in Subdivision, and Women's Exclusion (takhāruj)

Several methods have been developed to circumvent the laws of inheritance and skew them in favor of men. The most widespread method is to transfer real estate to male family members before the death of the owner. This is considered a sale and can potentially be viewed as an illegitimate transaction (*sūriat al bī'a*). The second way is to delay inheritance divisions, even over decades. The third is social pressure on women to renounce their rights.

Donations to Male Heirs before Death

Donations to sons while the owner is still alive are very common. This is specifically the case when the parents have only daughters to avoid the inheritance going to their own brothers or relatives. According to the DLS database, more than a third (37 percent) of land transactions in 2014 were conducted between close relatives (*usūl wa fughur*); between parents and children, between siblings, between husbands and wives. Over the years more and more sales are within the family: from a quarter of sales in 2005 to more than a third in 2014 (table 5.7). The share of sales between co-owners is also rising (*mushtarak*). DLS data do not show the gender of the buyer; rather, data indicate the widespread culture of selling land before death.

The justification commonly asserted for such sales is they confine the family property to male heirs, thereby preventing it from falling into the hands of the husbands of female relatives. Many fathers transfer their properties to their sons while still alive either by donating or selling property to them. Although Islamic laws forbid the transfer of more than a third of possessions before the death of the owner, few adhere to the laws. Indeed, most people give all their possessions and property to their sons—or to their brothers if the father only has daughters. This is the case both for Muslim and for Christian Jordanians: "It is local custom for Christian propertied patriarchs to give their main asset, land, to their sons as *premortem* inheritance, thus effectively disinheriting their daughters," according to Jansen (1993, 161).

In the case of the sale of possessions between family members, the DLS imposes a registration tax of 1 percent. A donation presents the risk that potential heirs at a later date will question its legality. Hence it is suggested by lawyers that possessions be sold to family members and not donated. As the DLS is only an implementing agency (*dā'ira tanfīthīya*) it is unable to intervene even if the decisions infringe on the law.[18] By contrast, only 15.7 percent of registered apartment sales were between family members in 2014, compared to 11.7 percent in 2005, but still low compared to land transactions (table 5.8). This is because registered apartments are built for profit, and their sale is a source of income. It is very likely that part of these apartments were "sold" to wives and children as protection against confiscation in case of bankruptcy.

There are two kinds of collective ownership: *musha'a*, where land is co-owned with other households, although with only one legal title for all the owners;

Table 5.7 Jordan Land Sale Patterns by Family Co-owners or Outsiders, 2005–2014

	2005		2014	
Land sales between co-owners (*mushtarak*)	2,641	2.8%	6,187	5.9%
Land sales to relatives (*usūl wa fughur*)	21,858	23.3%	38,926	37.1%
Normal land sales	69,321	73.9%	59,636	56.9%
Total sales	93,820	100%	104,749	100%

Source: Department of Land and Survey database prepared on request November 2015.

Rules on Paper, Rules in Practice • http://dx.doi.org/10.1596/978-1-4648-0886-9

Table 5.8 Apartment Sale Patterns by Family Co-owners or Outsiders, 2005–2014

	2005		2014	
Apartment sales between co-owners (*mushtarak*)	42	0.2%	169	0.4%
Apartment sales to relatives (*usūl wa fughur*)	2,165	11.7%	6,003	15.7%
Normal apartment sales	16,309	88.1%	32,146	83.9%
Total sales	18,516	100%	38,318	100%

Source: Department of Land and Survey database prepared on request November 2015.

or *mushtarak*, where several individuals buy a plot (most of the time of 250 m²) to be divided up. This type of ownership is common in the informal settlements of East Amman inhabited by Palestinian refugees. Most of the informal settlements in Jordan were upgraded in the 1980s. Most of their inhabitants hold *hujja* contracts, which are common throughout the Middle East. This involves the owner selling his land through the written agreement, the *hujja* (proof), after which the contract is named. This transaction is illegal and is not recognized by the DLS, but it does enable individuals to assert ownership over a property in a court (Razzaz 1991).

The Absence of Estate Division or Its Long Delay

A second technique used to deprive women of their shares in the inheritance is to prolong the time it takes to divide the land of the deceased. This permits the male relatives to organize ways to coerce the women into rejecting their share of the inheritance, providing compensation that falls short of the value of the women's shares in the property.

In 2010 the Jordanian National Forum for Women[19] conducted a major survey on the inheritance practices of women in the Irbid governorate.[20] Entitled *'ayn 'ala huqūq* (An Eye on the Rights) the survey was created within the framework of the "Equal Opportunities Support Program for Women and Girls". This survey was funded by the United Nations Population Fund and Oxfam Québec and it received technical assistance from the Jordanian Hashemite Fund for Human Development. The panel size consisted of women between ages 25–50 from 1,372 families distributed in all districts of Irbid governorate.[21]

The survey showed that the principal method used to deprive women of their rights is by forestalling the division of the inheritance between heirs. This is considered a public issue as the division of inheritance can be delayed for several years, which greatly affects women's inheritance rights and consequently their ability to enjoy any inheritance. The study revealed that 34 percent of women residing in the Irbid governorate did not receive their legal rights of inheritance (from 32.5 percent in Ramtha to 60.5 percent in Taybeh)[22] because of the absence of division. Indeed, the longer the division of inheritance is delayed, the more likely it is that a woman is deprived of her rights (Al Saheh 2010).

The status quo after the death of an estate owner is well established in matters of agricultural land. It can date back to a grandfather's death (in the 1950s and even earlier) and can be seen as an indication of the dominant patriarchal pattern of family life, in which everyone is aware of their share in the property. Therefore, official division or documentation is not required. According to a DLS engineer, there is no legal obligation to divide the property, and a familial arrangement will often suffice. This was the case before the British mandate, and these traditional means of controlling land were reinstated once the British left.[23]

The division of land or sale of apartment has a cost of 1 percent (*hujr al-ifrāz*) of its DLS–estimated value. Although this sum is low, some heirs would prefer not to pay it. This is particularly true for farmed land, and for apartments inhabited by a single female member (for example, a mother or an unmarried sister of the deceased). However, for the rest of the population, there is a need to sell and divide the estates, in particular for registered apartments that are viewed as investments. In 2004, the number of land divisions (*ifrāz*) was higher (12,615) than the number of inheritance cases (9,823) because of the multiplicity of plots. However, in the same year, the number of land divisions was nine times smaller than that of the 100,780 land sales (table 5.9).

As noticed by a lawyer at the DLS, one should not forget the importance of money compensation (*badal*) to exclusion.[24]

Social Pressure to Exclude Women from Property (takhāruj)

Women did not easily inherit land in Jordan before the 1990s. The patriarchal nature of Jordanian society has pushed women to renounce their inheritance in favor of their brothers or to be *"sheikha"* (a noble woman) and not utter a word on the matter. Women who refuse to waive their inheritance rights are threatened with abandonment and ostracism, and in the most extreme cases verbal abuse and physical violence. This is true for inheritance but also for all sales of

Table 5.9 Land Sales and Division Inheritance Procedures and Death by Gender, 2004

Governorate 2004	Land sale	Division (ifrāz)	Inheritance and exclusion	Male deaths	Female deaths	Total deaths
Amman	32,989	3,300	2,634	4,735	3,185	7,920
Balqa	5,897	581	602	475	342	817
Zarqa	9,985	939	844	1,314	903	2,217
Madaba	4,044	370	458	261	157	418
Irbid	16,747	4,071	2,114	1,688	1,235	2,923
Mafraq	10,140	1,345	653	381	231	612
Jerash	3,818	316	435	189	150	339
Ajlun	3,788	452	437	156	145	301
Kerak	6,510	726	815	354	272	626
Tafila	1,556	147	172	124	92	216
Maan	3,549	273	485	216	115	331
Aqaba	1,757	95	174	186	105	291
Kingdom	*100,780*	*12,615*	*9,823*	*10,079*	*6,932*	*17,011*

Source: Department of Land and Survey 2004 Yearbook table 48; Department of Statistics, Jordan Housing and Population Census 2004.

Rules on Paper, Rules in Practice • http://dx.doi.org/10.1596/978-1-4648-0886-9

land or apartments, as a transaction cannot be completed without the signature of all co-owners, including women. This is why pressure is often exerted on women either to give up the power of attorney or to renounce their share in a property.

According to the Jordanian National Forum for Women 2010 Survey on inheritance in Irbid, 20 percent of women renounced their inheritance rights: 15 percent willingly and 5 percent under pressure (Al Saheh 2010). In 2014 a third of heirs fully renounced their inheritance rights through *takhāruj*. That applied in 4,713 out of 17,264 inheritance cases (Sharia Supreme Court 2014). Although the gender of those who requested *takhāruj* has not been officially specified, surveys show most were women.

Donations of the third of the estate by the deceased (*wisayat*) to heirs and control over invalid heir shares (*waliyat*) were present in 6,425 cases, or 37 percent of all inheritance cases. However, the most impressive figure is the number of procurations asked from the Sharia Supreme Court: 9,208. This is explained by the fact that procurations are not always linked to inheritance, and they can be for other matters. It is interesting to note that over 2009–15, the percentage of each type stays rather stable, showing a constant trend in practices (figure 5.2).

In most governorates, the number of inheritance cases slightly exceeds the number of male deaths, as it includes the inheritance of women who possessed estates. In the major cities, such as Amman, the number of inheritance cases is smaller than the number of male deaths. This is due to the prevalence of

Figure 5.2 Inheritance, Exclusion, Power of Attorney, Will and Incapacity Cases—Sharia Supreme Court in Jordan (2009–14)

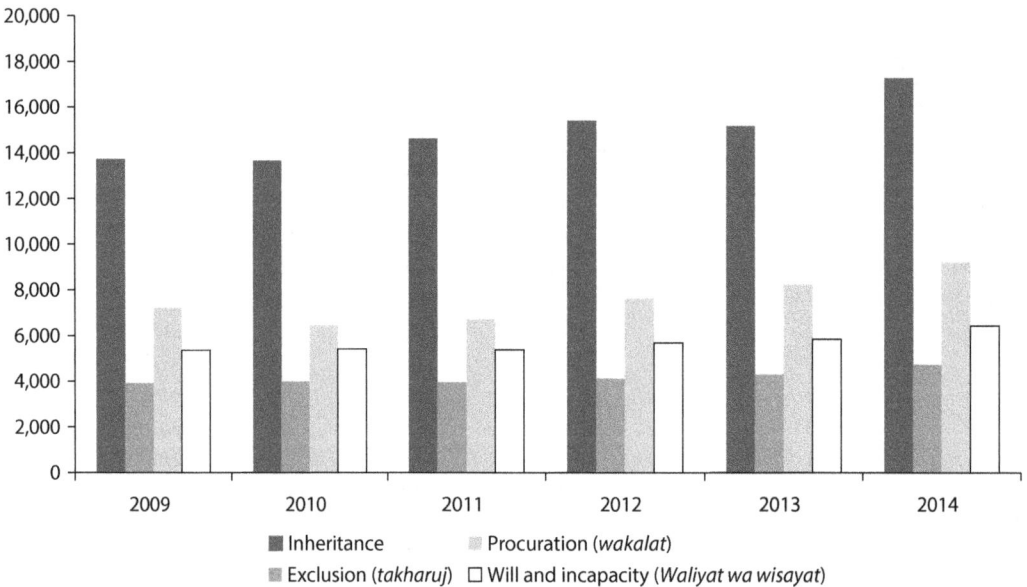

Sources: Sharia Supreme Court, Statistical Yearbook 2013 and 2014.

impoverished communities in the cities. In Zarqa, the number of inheritance cases is relatively low too, compared with the number of total deaths. The exclusion from property is high in Amman, Balqa, Madaba, and Maan. Zarqa governorate, which is highly urbanized, poor, and with little agricultural land, has the highest use of procurations and relatively less exclusion from inheritance than other governorates. Wills and incapacity procedures are used in more than half the inheritance cases heard in the governorates of Mafraq and Jerash.

Social Pressures on Women's Inheritance

"With love with will by force" (*fi mahabah fi ghida fi qūwwah*)
you will transfer to your brother![25]

"Shame on you! Why do you take from your brother his inheritance?"
(Ajlun governorate)[26]

Patriarchal norms are so deeply entrenched in Jordanian society that women themselves propagate them. Socially constrained, women believe that they have no right to inherit. The unity of the family and the continued support of its economic base constitute priorities in life and are deemed to be much more important than personal success. A woman who rebels against her brothers risks ostracism, which in turn would risk a damaging emotional and financial toll on her children. In this way, the subordination felt by women is often spread by women themselves, both in Muslim and in Christian families.[27]

Inheritance Rights Survey Opened a National Debate

The question of women's inheritance became a public debate in 2010 when the Jordanian National Forum for Women published the results of a major survey in several official newspapers (Al Saheh 2010). The survey showed that 74 percent of women who qualified to inherit land in Irbid governorate did not receive their inheritance rights in full. This was the case even as 91 percent of them were aware that these rights are guaranteed to them in accordance with Sharia law (Al Saheh 2010; Jordanian National Forum for Women 2010).

Only 15 percent of the surveyed women willingly gave up their right to inheritance. As for the rest, 34 percent of women in the survey did not receive their inheritance due to the division of the inheritance not taking place; 14 percent received less than what was rightfully theirs; 5 percent were forced to give up their right to inheritance; 4 percent did not receive it due to other problems; and 2 percent gave up their right to inheritance to avoid shame within the ethnic group. Only 26 percent of women in the survey who qualified for an inheritance received it in its totality.

It would appear that mourning is exploited to force women to give up their inheritance rights by invoking *takhāruj* (Al Saheh 2010).

Approximately half of the women (52 percent) who claimed their inheritance rights in the towns and villages of the Irbid governorate faced opposition. For 44 percent of them, this opposition came from their brothers; 22.5 percent stated that their mothers were the source of opposition; and 16.2 percent claimed that the father had stipulated how the inheritance should be distributed before his death and that within this the daughter should not receive her right to the inheritance (Al Saheh 2010).

Furthermore, the Jordanian National Forum for Women 2010 research indicates that young women were more successful in accessing full inheritance rights than elderly women. The percentage of those who received an incomplete inheritance in ages 45–50 was 18.9 percent, whereas for ages 25–29 it was 11.1 percent. Not one of the young women surveyed renounced their inheritance rights out of fear of bringing shame to their family by disobeying tribal laws. This can be credited to societal development over the past 25 years in general awareness and education, besides the weakening influence of customs and traditions within this age group (Al Saheh 2010).

According to the study, unemployed women are considered the most perspicacious with regard to matters of inheritance, since 37.2 percent of unemployed women received their full rights. Only 26.9 percent of working women received their inheritance in full. The percentage was lower for women who were not active in the economy, at 23.1 percent. This is due to the consideration given by brothers to female family members who lack stable sources of income (Al Saheh 2010).

Marriage status affects the likelihood of receiving full inheritance rights. Of the women who received their full inheritance rights in the 2010 survey, unmarried women represented 37.9 percent, whereas only 24.3 percent were married. Two reasons can explain this. The first is that if an unmarried girl dies all the assets go to her family; the second reason is the commonly held belief that the daughter's husband should not receive the father's inheritance (Al Saheh 2010).

Paradoxically endogamy (40 percent of weddings in Jordan are between first or second cousins) (DOS and ICF 2013) does not guarantee better inheritance opportunities. From the survey, it is evident that women who are related to their husbands are less likely to receive inheritance (24.3 percent against 37.9 percent) whereas 30.5 percent of women who are not related to their husbands realize their inheritance.

The study called for campaigns to increase awareness of the rights to inheritance through various methods, including the use of media channels and cooperation with mosques to emphasize that it is religiously illegitimate to deny women their legal rights. If some contested its methodology, even the most conservative agreed that the recommendations were most valid.[28]

Social Pressure and Embarrassment

Significant pressure is exerted on women who do not agree with the decisions to dissuade them from taking the matter to court. This action is further supported by an unwritten social norm that condemns taking out a lawsuit against one's brother. Social norms often deter women from seeking justice through the legal system out of fear of being excluded or exposed to physical violence.

Pursuing a legal claim to inheritance is costly and difficult for women if male family members are reluctant to cooperate. When a woman choses to go to court, she must have financial assets because court costs in Jordan can reach 8 percent of the value of the claim, which is higher than in all other Middle East countries.[29]

Women must be supported by relatives as in the Sharia court the testimony of two women is equal to that of one man. "The social norms of the Jordanian patriarchy continue to prevail hindering women from practicing their rights on an equal footing with men. This paves the way for rising cases of violence against women," according to the Human Forum for Women's Rights (2007). The Justice Center for Legal Aid, Jordan's largest legal aid provider, reports that 70 percent of the cases it assists are on the request of women.

According to the Statistical Survey on the Volume of Demand for Legal Aid conducted by the DOS with support of the World Bank in 2012, and featuring 10,000 households, women were nearly four times as likely as men to be involved in a dispute about personal status issues—41 percent of women versus 11 percent of men (Prettitore 2013). "Poor women were almost ten times as likely to request counseling for personal status issues. Women are less likely to find amicable solutions for their disputes. Almost 40 percent of men reporting disputes in the LAS solved them amicably, while only just over 30 percent of women were able to do the same. This suggests men may have greater access to informal means of dispute resolution, for example through family and business contacts, and that perhaps women's restricted agency in social, economic and political life reduces their potential networks" (Prettitore 2013).

An educated woman from Al Hisa, a small city in Tafilah governorate, was ostracized by her six brothers when she decided to convince her five sisters to defend their inheritance rights after the death of their father in 2014. The elder son wanted to sell the house where the mother was living, although his father had built a house for each of his sons. The mother was intimidated and did not want to explain to her sons that she would prefer to stay in her house instead of living with one of her stepdaughters. In her words: "They do not want girls to inherit." In response to her daughter's actions, the mother called her to thank her and to confirm her support for her daughter.[30]

With the advances in education and improved awareness of women's rights examples like this are becoming less common. An example of this is the case of the well-established Christian family of Al Haddadin from which one of Jordan's Chief of Appeal Court came. When Issa Haddadin, a Christian landlord owning estates in Ma'in near Madaba, passed away in 1937 he deprived his daughters from their share of the inheritance. He had one handicapped son and three girls from a first marriage, and one son and one daughter from a second marriage. One of his first three daughters Rahma married Khalil Al Haddadin. When he died in 1994 their seven sons and four daughters received legally their full shares of the inheritance. Each woman received approximately 85 donums.[31]

It seems that women in Amman are more eager to defend their inheritance rights, as they are more aware of them and a high number of them are working.

The Risk of Losing Male Guardianship (qawama)

"Hammāt al-banāt la'l mamāt"

("Taking care of women is a problem until death")

Jordanian misogynistic idiom, November 2015.

Male guardianship of female family members is not only a tradition but is inscribed in the law. According to the Jordanian Personal Status Law No. 36 of 2010 (articles 14 and 15) a male blood relative (*wāli*) has the right to have guardianship of women. If a woman is unmarried and under age 30 or previously was married, she must have a male guardian. Upon marriage a woman is transferred from her father's custody to her husband. In Jordan women's rights to housing continues to be connected to her status as a wife or a daughter. If the father dies the brothers have the right to sell the house in which their mother and sister(s) are living. Consequently, the fate of the women depends on the quality of the relationships that they have with male members of their family. In the event of divorce, a woman only has a right to housing if "she is nursing or has been granted custody of the children" (Al Husseini 2010).

Due to their lack of economic independence, Jordanian divorced or widowed women are in dire straits if they have no family support, or if they have been ostracised while protesting during inheritance. In 2012, half of divorced women had to work. Two-thirds of widows had no other solution than to work, whereas only one-third of widowed men were working. Divorced or widowed women lead 85.7 percent of the poor households headed by women, whereas only 0.6 percent of poor households are headed by divorced or widowed men (DOS and KVINFO 2012, 53).

Mobilization for Enforcing Women's Inheritance Rights

Women's rights activists have to find ways of action within the framework of the Sharia law, which constitutes a red line in Jordan's conservative society. Their success is remarkable. In 2009, they managed to gain the right for women to choose their residence.[32] In 2010, women's rights activists succeeded in amending the Jordanian Personal Status Law No. 36 of 2010 by working with the Supreme Sharia Court (Qadi al-Quda), the highest religious and legal institution in Jordan. The result was seven amendments to the law, and the introduction of Articles 318 and 319 on property and exclusion.

Sharia Supreme Court Measures to Protect the Inheritance Rights of Women

The seven amendments to the Personal Law No. 36 of 2010 Articles 318 and 319 were introduced on the demand of the Sharia Supreme Court in 2011.[33] The first set a mandatory period of three months after the death of the owner before either exclusion or power of attorney can be invoked.

The amendment was adopted to give women time before declaring their rejection of inheritance rights. This enables women to deal with the grief caused by the loss of a parent and means that they do not have to concern themselves with making important decisions while in a vulnerable emotional state. This in turn reduces the possibility of women being coerced by their brothers into renouncing their inheritance rights. The second amendment states that judges must inform all heirs of the consequences of exclusion procedures. This has resulted in judges asking for better education for women so that they are able to defend their rights. The fourth amendment states that the attorney is under obligation to inform the heirs of all the properties included in an inheritance. The sixth amendment prohibits invoking the power of attorney (*waqālat*) during the first three months after the death of the owner. All these measures were taken to protect the rights of the heirs, especially the rights of women.[34]

To limit general exclusion, higher fees were introduced in August 2015. Limited exclusion from inheritance costs only JD10, whereas general exclusion now costs JD15 per heir. Before higher fees were introduced, the fee for exclusion was 2 percent of the amount inherited. However, this resulted in false declarations. When judges wanted to study the inheritance procedure they noticed that it was impossible to have an accurate understanding of inheritance as the financial value of the inherited possessions was severely understated (around JD50 to JD200 on average per case). In order to provide an honest representation of the system of inheritance, heirs are now asked to write the precise amount that they receive.

The Jordanian Civil Law guarantees women financial independence and protects them from coercion. Article 141 guarantees the rejection of deals and contracts that have be reached through coercion. Article 142 provides "special protection to woman in facing their husband who forces them to relinquish rights or property" (Jordanian National Forum for Women 2012).

Another legislative measure is the ability to prevent a sale made by a dying person to an heir unless it is approved by all heirs (Paragraph 1 of Article 544 of the Jordanian Civil Law). To protect all the heirs, paragraph (b) of Article 274 of the Provisional Jordanian Personal Status Law No. 36 of 2010 forbids enforcement of a will that exceeds one-third of the inheritance. However, the problem is that in many cases the donation was made by the elder owner and no action can be taken.

One of the recommendations of the Jordanian National Commission for Women (2010) is to amend Article 279 of the Provisional Jordanian Personal Status Law number 36 of 2010 in order to grant rights to a mandated will to the children of a deceased daughter similar to the right granted to the children of a deceased son. This is a major issue, as not only women are not inheriting, but their children too are deprived of any inheritance. It calls also for a clear statement to regulate "farar divorce," which is the divorce of a wife incurred by a dying husband in order to deprive his wife of her right to inherit from him when he dies. The statement should allow a wife in such a situation to inherit though divorced by a dying husband (JNCW 2010 p. 28).

Women's rights defenders are also helping women access their full dowries at their husband's death, such as the legal NGO Mizan does.[35] Few women are aware of their rights to obtain the remainder of their dowry after the death of their husband before any of the division of inheritance occurs. In Jordan, marriage contracts require two payments: one prior to the wedding (*al-mu'ajal*) and one after the wedding (*al-muajal*). Women often receive this second payment in the eventuality of a divorce. The monetary value of the second payment is often much greater. Lower-middle-class women will be married with 2,500 to 5,000 JD (including gold), which is paid to her before the wedding, and double this amount in the case of divorce. A middle-class woman will agree to marry for a symbolic dinar in gold, but the judge will protect her rights by stipulating an amount in case of divorce (from 5,000 to 15,000 JD and in some cases more).

Conclusion

In Jordan, immovable property is a male domain. Land is the major source of family wealth for large segments of society, both in rural areas and within cities. Traditionally land has been considered a source of income for men with which they take care of their family. Although women's rights to inheritance are guaranteed by Sharia law, men are reluctant to give land shares to female children who will become part of the husband's family once married. This male line of wealth transmission is true both for private land and agricultural land and for both Muslim and Christian families.

Jordan is a conservative country when it comes to women's rights. Most of the rights are indeed written and subject to public debate. But the fact is that women are locked in multilayered structures that reinforce each other in society, patriarchal order, religion, and traditions. Male guardianship (*qawama*) is used as a justification not to give their rights to women because of its high costs.

Property and inheritance rights and practices are revealing social and cultural interactions. They reveal domination patterns that impede women's social participation to the economy. In Jordan, girls are not inheriting property on equal terms with theirs brothers on the pretext that they will be married and that their husband will have to provide a house. Gender–based restrictions on women's legal capacity and property rights are still prevalent in Jordan. Men have developed strategies not to give women their rights, such as delaying the division of an estate after the death of the father.

In Jordan, the three sources of women's economic autonomy are all restricted. The first with regard to financial value is inheritance. However, as we have seen, several techniques are employed to deprive women of this. The second is the dowry. However, only half is received upon marriage, and the remainder is received at divorce or death. In the worst cases, the husband takes complete control of the dowry, denying the wife access. The third is employment, but the labor participation rate for women in Jordan is one of the lowest in the world, 15 percent in the formal sector and only 22 percent in the informal sector. Furthermore, women do not have freedom of choice with regard to the sector in which they work. Society in general is accepting of women working in the public sector, but not in the private sector, where she could be exposed to sexual harassment.

Paradoxically the gradual increase in the dominance of conservative religious views in Jordanian society has a positive consequence when it comes to pushing for the implementation of Sharia law in matters of inheritance. Statistics and surveys tend to show a slight improvement in women's inheritance patterns in Jordan over the past 25 years. This is due not only to women's increased awareness of their rights but also to stronger Islamic conservatism that encourages men to implement "God's will" with regard to women's rights. Social norms regarding inheritance are progressively moving in Jordan, but at a slow pace. Enhanced inheritance would help women to break the glass ceiling that limits their economic assets. It would improve their capacity to engage in paid activities. This is even more needed given that Jordan lags behind only Saudi Arabia in its lack of incentives for women to work (World Bank 2013b).

Notes

1. The Global Land Tool Network, facilitated by UN Habitat. http://www.gltn.net /index.php/land-tools/cross-cutting-issues/islamic-aspects.

2. According to a survey conducted by S. J. Nasir: Nasir. 1969. "Working Women in the Changing Society of Jordan." Survey by the Faculty of Arts Journal (Jordan University, Amman) in Jansen 1993, 165. This is important, as most surveys do not include this major religious dimension.

3. This document is issued in one day and costs JD1.5.

4. The total population of Jordan could be as high at 9.5 million people, according to the preliminary results of the National Housing and Population Census 2015, and includes 1.265 million Syrian refugees (639,000 registered by United Nations High Commission for Refugees). Bishop Maroun Lahham, Latin Patriarchal Vicar of Jordan, estimates Christians in Jordan to number about 250,000, in his book *Al-Urdun: Târikh wa-imân wa-jamâl. Al-niyâba al-batrîyarkiya al-lâtiniya al-'âma fi-l-urdun*, 2015 (Maroun Lahham, *Jordan: History, Faith and Beauty* [2015]).

5. In 1922, British Mandate authorities introduced a provision on inheritance rights for Christians. Inspired by Western civil law, it stipulated that girls and boys should inherit equal shares. The 1951 family law of independent Jordan abolished this text and referred each church to its own canon. However, no church canon provided clauses concerning the distribution of shares of an inheritance, stipulating rather that the civil law of the country should apply (Chatelard 2004).

6. As anthropological works have shown (Chatelard 2004; Jansen 1993), a frequent practice among Muslims and Christians alike is to deprive girls of the half share on inheritance accorded to them under Sharia. Based on e-mail correspondence with Dr. Géraldine Chatelard, social anthropologist, December 1, 2015.

7. Interview with Dr. A. Al Omari, a judge at the Sharia Supreme Court, November 4, 2015.

8. According to Amal Haddadin, lawyer at the Jordanian National Commission for Women and main author of the CEDAW country report on Jordan, November 1, 2015.

9. Communal land exploitation (*musha'a*) represented 82 percent of land in the governorate of Ajlun; 22 percent in Balqa; and 26 percent in Kerak, and did not exist in Ma'an. Privately owned land (*mafrūz*) prevailed in the central regions of Balqa in Kerak and in Ma'an. In general, olive groves and orchards tended to be privately owned. It was the role of the sheikhs to oversee the yearly allocation of *musha'a* land shares (Fischbach 2000, 68).

10. See the DOS, Agriculture Census 2007, table 1.2.

11. Regulation of the size of land divided between co-owners No. 70, 2001. *Nizam al masaha al mafrūza bayn al shuraka*. Some landowners are currently putting pressure on the DLS to have this brought down to 2 donums, which would be an easier plot to sell for building on near the cities and villages.

12. The rulers of the Ottoman Empire, who controlled much of the Middle East during the 19th century, tried to make most of land either *waqf* or *miri*. While this restricted land fragmentation and curbed the powers of large landowners and tribal chiefs, the long-term consequence of the increase of *waqf* land was the immobilization of city land (cited in Payne 1996).

13. See the HUDC 2004, Base line survey, Community Infrastructure Program A.

14. Interview with the head of the DLS Legal Affairs, November 5, 2015.

15. Or they do not provide it to researchers.

16. Data provided to the author by the head of the Information System at the Department of Land and Survey, November 11, 2015.

17. DOS Gender Statistics, given to the author in October 2015.

18. Interview with lawyer H. B., Legal Affairs, Department of Land and Surveys November 5, 2015.

19. The Jordanian National Forum for Women is a nongovernment organization established in 1995 that seeks to advance the position of women in society throughout Jordan. This is achieved through programs intended to raise awareness of the issues faced by women; offering training, capacity-building programs, and other assistance; and establishing projects that encourage the adoption of principles of equality and equal opportunities. Furthermore, the organization strives to find methods to increase women's participation in decisions and to empower them so that they might engage more in public life.

20. The Irbid Governorate in Jordan's northwest has about 1.1 million people.

21. During our visit of the Jordanian National Forum for Women only a two-page leaflet was presented. The following statistics and analysis are translated from an article published in Arabic in the Al Dustour government-owned newspaper on September 26, 2010 (Al Saheh 2010).

22. Ramtha (32.1 percent), Bani 'Ubayd (34 percent), Al Kura (38.3 percent), Al Mazar Al-Shamali (38.6 percent), Bani Kinana (39 percent), and At Tayba (60.5 percent). At Tayba district has the highest score for women's knowledge of their inheritance rights (98 percent) and the highest percentage among districts with women who have not got their inheritance right in the inheritance division (60.5 percent). This demonstrates that the link between a woman's knowledge of the inheritance right and actually achieving her right is not always very strong (Al Saheh 2010).

23. Interview with A. S., head of public relations at the DLS, November 24, 2015. He stated the case of his wife whose grandfather owned 150 donums in the village of Huwwara, near Irbid, shared across three plots of 50 donums each. Her grandfather

passed away in the 1950s, but only one of the plots was divided and shared out among the children and grandchildren to build their houses. However, the other two plots remained under the control of the elder sons (*musha'a*).

24. Based on an interview with the Department of Land and Surveys, November 24, 2015.

25. Dr. Abeer Dababneh director of the Center for Women's Studies University of Jordan, October 28, 2015.

26. "'Ayb! Leysh tākhūdh min wirth akhūk?" is from an interview with a woman from Deir Smadi, October 28, 2015, in the Amman Center for Women Studies.

27. "The president of the Latin ecclesiastical court in Amman echoed the sentiments of women from Madaba: "Even today among Christians a woman who marries is automatically disinherited and she finds that natural. It is the tradition and people do not question it." (Taken from an interview with Father Ghaleb Bader in 1995 (Abu Sneineh 2014).

28. Interviews at the Sharia Supreme Court, November 2015.

29. "Based on the indicator "Enforcement of Contracts" in the World Bank's Doing Business Report 2012, costs as a percentage of the value of the claim are as follows: Jordan–8 percent; Syria–4.5 percent; Lebanon–3 percent; Iraq–2.3 percent; West Bank and Gaza–2.2 percent; and Egypt–1.3 percent" (World Bank 2013a, 79).

30. Interview at the Jordan National Forum for Women, November 1, 2015.

31. According to Amal Haddadin, lawyer at the Jordanian National Commission for Women, November 1, 2015.

32. Women's rights campaigners managed to have the reservation regarding Article 15/4 (which states that "the wife must reside with her husband") of the Convention on the Elimination of All Forms of Violence Against Women (CEDAW) removed in March 2009.

33. *Ta'limat tanzim wa tasjil hujaj al-takhāruj li sana*, 2011 Official Journal 5067, January 16, 2011.

34. Interview with Dr. A. Al Omari, judge at the Sharia Supreme Court, November 4, 2015.

35. Interview with lawyer Eva Abu Halaweh, November 1, 2015.

References

Ababsa,Myriam. 2012. "Public Policies toward Informal Settlements in Jordan (1965–2009)." In *Popular Housing and Urban Land Tenure in the Middle East: Case Studies from Egypt, Syria, Jordan, Lebanon, and Turkey,* edited by Myriam Ababsa, Eric Denis, and Baudouin Dupret, 259–82. Cairo: American University in Cairo Press.

———. 2013. *Atlas of Jordan. History Territories and Society.* Beirut: IFPO 485. http://books.openedition.org/ifpo/4560.

Abujaber, Raouf Sa'd. 1989. *Pioneers over Jordan: The Frontier of Settlement in Transjordan, 1850–1914.* London: I. B. Tauris.

Abu Sneineh, Abdulrahman. 2014. "Disinheritance of Women Legalized." *Arab Reporters for Investigative Journalism, Al Ghad.* http://en.arij.net/report/disinheritance-of-women-legalized/.

Al Husseini, Rana. 2010. "Jordan." In *Women's Rights in the Middle East and North Africa: Progress Amid Resistance*, edited by Sanja Kelly and Julia Breslin, 192–222. New York: Freedom House. http://www.freedomhouse.org.

Al Saheh, Iman. 2010. "A Study Reveals That 74% of Women in the Governorate of Irbid Do Not Receive Their Full Rights to Inheritance." *Al Dustour*, September, 26, 2010 (in Arabic). http://www.addustour.com.

Baer, Gabriel. 1957. "Land Tenure in the Hashemite Kingdom of Jordan." *Land Economics* 33 (8): 187–97.

Chatelard, Géraldine. 2004. *Briser la Mosaïque: Les Tribus Chrétiennes de Madaba*. Paris: CNRS Éditions.

COHRE (Centre on Housing Rights and Evictions). 2006. *In Search of Equality: A Survey of Law and Practice Related to Women's Inheritance Rights in the Middle East and North Africa (MENA) Region*. Geneva.

DOS and ICF (ICF International). 2013. *Jordan Population and Family Health Survey 2012*. Department of Statistics, Amman; ICF International, Calverton, MD, 350. https://dhsprogram.com/pubs/pdf/FR282/FR282.pdf.

DOS and KVINFO (Danish Center for Research on Women and Gender). 2012. "Woman and Man in Jordan: A Statistical Portrait." The Danish Centre for Information on Gender Equality and Ethnicity, Department of Statistics, Amman, 101.

Fischbach, Michael R. 2000. *State, Society and Land in Jordan*. Leiden, The Netherlands: Brill.

HKJ (Hashemite Kingdom of Jordan). 2013. "Needs Assessment Review of the Impact of the Syrian Crisis on Jordan." Report prepared with the United Nations.

———. 2014. National Report for the Preparation of UN-Habitat III.

HUDC (Housing and Urban Development Corporation). 2004. "CIP-A Completion Report." Unpublished report.

Jansen, Willy. 1993. "Creating Identities: Gender, Religion and Women's Property in Jordan." In *Who's Afraid of Feminity? Questions of Identity*, edited by M. Brugman, et al., 157–67. Amsterdam: Rodopi.

JNCW (Jordanian National Commission for Women). 2010. *Jordan's Fifth National Periodic Report to the CEDAW Committee—Summary*. Jordanian National Commission for Women, Amman, 32. http://www.women.jo/admin/document/CEDAW%20English.pdf.

———. 2012. *Women's Rights to Inheritance: Realities and Proposed Policies*. (In Arabic, p. 21, and in English, p. 28). http://www.johud.org.jo/SystemFiles/SSfile_635143893539732903.pdf.

Payne, Geoffrey. 1996. *Urban Land Tenure and Property Rights in Developing Countries: A Review of the Literature*. London: Overseas Development Administration, 86.

Prettitore, Paul. 2013. *Gender and Justice in Jordan: Women, Demand and Access*. World Bank, MENA Knowledge and Learning Quick Notes Series no. 107, 4. Washington, DC: World Bank.

Razzaz, Omar. 1991. "Law Urban Land Tenure and Property Disputes in Contested Settlements: The Case of Jordan." PhD dissertation, Harvard University.

———. 1996. "Land Conflicts Property Rights and Urbanization East of Amman." In *Amman Ville et Société: The City and Its Society*, edited by Jean Hannoyer and Seteney Shami, 499–526. Amman: CERMOC.

Sharia Supreme Court. 2014. *Statistical Yearbook 2014: Dairat Qadi al Quda, Taqrir al Ihsai al Sanawi li 'am,* 2014, 245.

World Bank. 2005. *The Economic Advancement of Women in Jordan: A Country Gender Assessment: Social and Economic Development Group.* Washington, DC: World Bank, 160.

———. 2013a. *The Hashemite Kingdom of Jordan: Jordan Country Gender Assessment; Economic Participation, Agency and Access to Justice in Jordan.* Washington, DC: World Bank, 99.

———. 2013b. *Women, Business and the Law 2014: Removing Restrictions to Enhance Gender Equality.* Washington, DC: World Bank, 192.

Regional Comparisons Along Eight Dimensions of the WJP Rule of Law Index

For a better understanding of rule-of-law outcomes in the Middle East and North Africa (MENA) and other developing regions, we provide here a brief summary of the scores for eight of the nine dimensions of the World Justice Project (WJP) rule-of-law measure. No empirical measures exist for WJP Factor 9, Informal Justice.

Factor 1: Limited Government Powers

As described in chapter 1, in many developing countries—especially ones with autocratic or hybrid regimes—elites and governing elites are often not subject to the same laws as everyone else. The WJP limited government powers factor examines one aspect of this phenomenon. (We examine more below.) Namely, it "measures the extent to which those who govern are subject to law" (World Justice Project 2011, 10). That is, how accountable are government officials to the population and to what extent are their powers limited by law?

Table A.1 presents regional and income average Factor 1 scores, using the same World Bank classification system adopted throughout this book. Starting from the last column, we notice first that all of the developing regions score much lower than the developed group—by almost 30 points. MENA stands out in that it performs best among the developing regions. The average for the lower-middle income countries, the Arab Republic of Egypt and Morocco, is the highest for all developing regions and nine percentage points above the average for the income group. For the upper-middle income countries, the Islamic Republic of Iran, Jordan, Lebanon, and Tunisia, MENA do better than the other higher-income Europe and Central Asia (ECA) and East Asia and Pacific (EAP) countries but worse than Latin America and Caribbean (LAC) and the average of Botswana and South Africa. In all, it is about average. The score for Factor 1 in

Table A.1 WJP Factor 1—Limited Government Powers

Region	Income				
	Lower	Lower middle	Upper middle	High	Total
MNA	...	**0.57**	**0.52**	**0.55**	**0.54**
		2	**4**	**1**	**7**
ECA	0.44	0.39	0.46	0.69	0.51
	1	5	9	6	21
EAP	0.34	0.52	0.49	0.66	0.51
	1	4	3	1	9
LAC		0.43	0.54	...	0.51
		4	12		16
SSA	0.45	0.50	0.68	...	0.49
	10	6	2		18
SAR	0.45	0.54	...	...	0.51
	2	3			5
DEV	...	...	...	0.80	0.80
				21	21
Total	0.44	0.48	0.52	0.77	0.57
	14	24	30	29	97

Note: MNA = Middle East and North Africa; ECA = Europe and Central Asia; EAP = East Asia and Pacific;
LAC = Latin America and the Caribbean; SSA = Sub-Saharan Africa; and DEV = developed countries.
... = no observations for that category.

the United Arab Emirates is very low, even lower than the score for the MENA lower-middle income group. Furthermore, it is 25 percentage points below the score for all countries classified as developed (DEV) and 20 percentage points below the average for all high income countries. In all, MENA appears to be very similar to other regions—with slightly stronger results for the lower-middle income countries, Morocco and Egypt.

Factor 2: Absence of Corruption

Corruption is another means by which the rule of law is not achieved, as it allows business and governing elites to benefit more than the rest of population. Factor 2 examines "three forms of corruption: bribery, improper influence by public or private interests, and misappropriation of public funds or other resources" (World Justice Project 2011, 12) in all three branches of government.

The absence of corruption is highly correlated with income—with corruption falling as income rises. Within income groups, MENA performs best in the lower-middle income group and performs better than average in the upper-middle income group. The United Arab Emirates also performs well for this factor. Although it is below the average, which is strongly affected by the high average for the developed regions (marked DEV in table A.2), it has the same score as the Republic of Korea and scores 7 percentage points better than the average of the high income European Union (EU) countries.

Table A.2 WJP Factor 2—Absence of Corruption

Region	Income				
	Lower	Lower middle	Upper middle	High	Total
MNA	...	**0.42**	**0.50**	**0.74**	**0.51**
		2	**4**	**1**	**7**
ECA	0.26	0.39	0.47	0.67	0.50
	1	5	9	6	21
EAP	0.31	0.38	0.54	0.74	0.47
	1	4	3	1	9
LAC	...	0.34	0.48	...	0.45
		4	12		16
SSA	0.38	0.37	0.63	...	0.40
	10	6	2		18
SAR	0.34	0.37	...	...	0.36
	2	3			5
DEV	...	...	...	0.83	0.83
				21	21
Total	0.36	0.38	0.50	0.79	0.53
	14	24	30	29	97

Note: MNA = Middle East and North Africa; ECA = Europe and Central Asia; EAP = East Asia and Pacific;
LAC = Latin America and the Caribbean; SSA = Sub-Saharan Africa; and DEV = developed countries.
... = no observations for that category.

Consequently, MENA has the highest average score among all developing regions, regardless of income.

Factor 3: Order and Security

WJP defines order and security as "how well the society assures the security of persons and property. It encompasses three dimensions: absence of crime; absence of civil conflict, including terrorism and armed conflict; and absence of violence as a socially acceptable means to redress personal grievances" (World Justice Project 2011, 12).

As expected, MENA scores very high on Factor 3 across all income groups, with a total average score of 0.74. It is not alone in this regard, however. Countries in Europe and Central Asia and East Asia and Pacific score just as high, at 0.76 and 0.74 averages, respectively. Latin America and the Caribbean and Africa are substantially lower at 0.60 and 0.62 averages, respectively, while South Asia has the lowest average score, at 0.51. Another interesting point is the particularly high score of the United Arab Emirates. At 0.91, the United Arab Emirates is higher than the average for the developed regions, at 0.85.

Figure A.1 presents a listing of the scores for several countries on subfactor 3.1 (Is crime effectively controlled?), which gives us a sense of the variability among countries within country-region groups. For example, Jordan scores much higher

Table A.3 WJP Factor 3—Order and Security

| Region | Income | | | | |
	Lower	Lower Middle	Upper Middle	High	Total
MNA	...	**0.70**	**0.73**	**0.91**	**0.74**
		2	**4**	**1**	**7**
ECA	0.74	0.79	0.72	0.81	0.76
	1	5	9	6	21
EAP	0.70	0.72	0.76	0.82	0.74
	1	4	3	1	9
LAC	...	0.62	0.60	...	0.60
		4	12		16
SSA	0.62	0.61	0.66	...	0.62
	10	6	2		18
SAR	0.65	0.41	...	...	0.51
	2	3			5
DEV	...	...	...	0.85	0.85
				21	21
Total	0.64	0.65	0.67	0.84	0.71
	14	24	30	29	97

Note: MNA = Middle East and North Africa; ECA = Europe and Central Asia; EAP = East Asia and Pacific;
LAC = Latin America and the Caribbean; SSA = Sub-Saharan Africa; and DEV = developed countries.
... = no observations for that category.

Figure A.1 WJP Factor 3—Order and Security

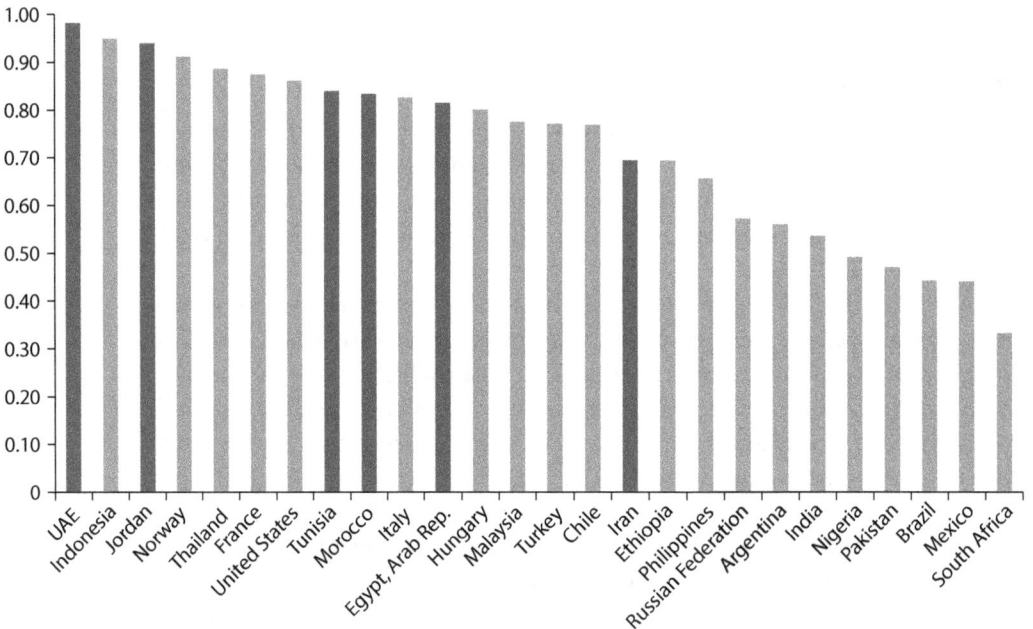

Note: UAE = United Arab Emirates

than the Islamic Republic of Iran. The high scores for MENA countries are particularly striking.

Factor 4: Fundamental Rights

Factor 4 assesses the protection of fundamental human rights. It covers the effective protection of freedom of expression, religion, privacy, assembly, fundamental labor rights, and due process under law, and so on (World Justice Project 2011, 12).

MENA scores very low on this factor. It posts the lowest score across all income groups. Moreover, whereas European and Central Asian countries and those in East Asia and Pacific show large increases in fundamental rights moving from upper-middle income to high income, no such increase occurs in MENA. The score for the United Arab Emirates is even lower than the upper-middle income average. The average for all MENA countries, at 0.48, is more than 30 percentage points below the developed regions average of 0.81.

Factor 5: Open Government

WJP measures open government by the extent to which laws are clearly written and made public, and the extent to which the public is able to participate in the formation and administration of laws (for example, through petitions and public consultations).

Table A.4 WJP Factor 4—Fundamental Rights

Region	Income				
	LOW	L_MID	U_MID	HI	Total
MNA	...	0.45	0.50	0.47	0.48
		2	4	1	7
ECA	0.51	0.54	0.58	0.77	0.62
	1	5	9	6	21
EAP	0.43	0.56	0.50	0.76	0.55
	1	4	3	1	9
LAC	...	0.55	0.63		0.61
		4	12	...	16
SSA	0.50	0.52	0.62	...	0.52
	10	6	2		18
SAR	0.51	0.52		...	0.52
	2	3	...		5
DEV	...	...	...	0.81	0.81
				21	21
Total	0.50	0.53	0.58	0.79	0.62
	14	24	30	29	97

Note: MNA = Middle East and North Africa; ECA = Europe and Central Asia; EAP = East Asia and Pacific; LAC = Latin America and the Caribbean; SSA = Sub-Saharan Africa; and DEV = developed countries. ... = no observations for that category.

Table A.5 WJP Factor 5—Open Government

Region	Income				
	Low	Lower middle	Upper middle	High	Total
MNA	...	0.50	0.44	0.44	0.46
		2	4	1	7
ECA	0.44	0.43	0.46	0.58	0.49
	1	5	9	6	21
EAP	0.37	0.42	0.47	0.74	0.47
	1	4	3	1	9
LAC	...	0.43	0.50	...	0.49
		4	12		16
SSA	0.37	0.39	0.64	...	0.41
	10	6	2		18
SAR	0.37	0.44	...	...	0.41
	2	3			5
DEV	...	...	...	0.76	0.76
				21	21
Total	0.38	0.43	0.49	0.71	0.52
	14	24	30	29	97

Note: MNA = Middle East and North Africa; ECA = Europe and Central Asia; EAP = East Asia and Pacific; LAC = Latin America and the Caribbean; SSA = Sub-Saharan Africa; and DEV = developed countries. ... = no observations for that category.

Results for Factor 5 follow a similar pattern to the results for Factor 4: whereas the score for other regions increases as we move to higher income groups, the score for MENA does not. Instead, although lower-middle income countries the Arab Republic of Egypt and Morocco outperform the rest of the lower-middle income category, the upper-middle income and high income countries post the lowest scores in their respective income groups. The score of the United Arab Emirates in the high income group is especially low.

Figure A.2 highlights the variability of scores within country-region groups—for example, Jordan scores much higher than Lebanon—and shows the tendency for MENA countries to score lower than the average for the upper-middle income and high income countries.

Factor 6: Regulatory Enforcement

As described in chapter 1, selective regulatory enforcement is a key tool used by governing elites to control society and to reward supporters and punish enemies. WJP ranks countries on this factor by "how well regulations are implemented and enforced" and it goes on to say: "This includes the absence of improper influence by public officials or private interests; adherence to administrative procedures that are fair, consistent, and predictable; and freedom from government taking of private property without adequate compensation" (World Justice Project 2011, 13).

Figure A.2 WJP Subfactor 5.1

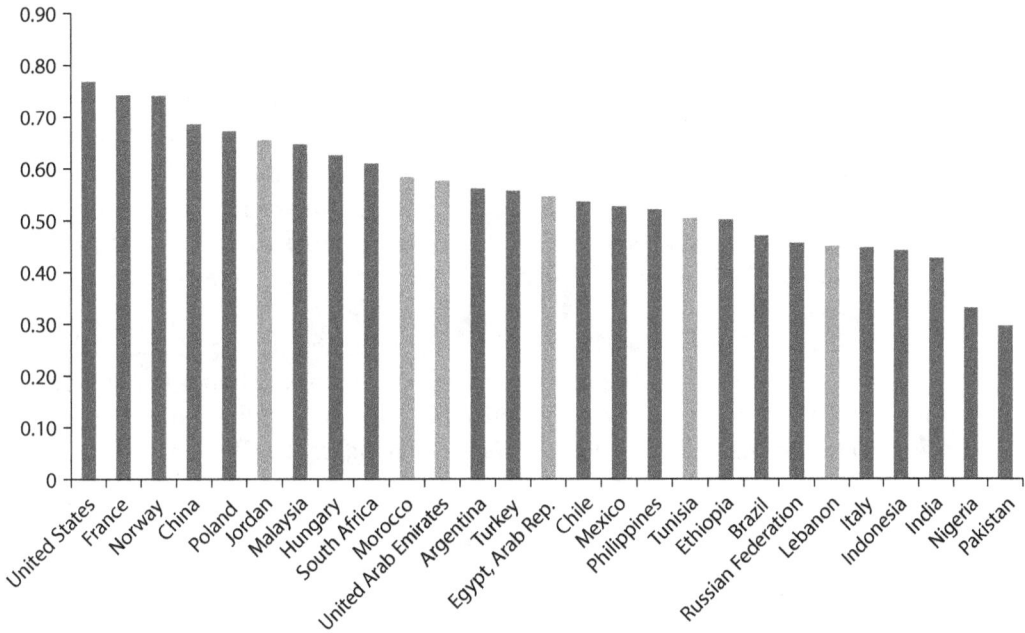

Table A.6 WJP Factor 6—Regulatory Enforcement

Region	Income				
	Low	Lower Middle	Upper Middle	High	Total
MNA	...	0.44	0.51	0.65	0.51
		2	4	1	7
ECA	0.43	0.45	0.51	0.60	0.52
	1	5	9	6	21
EAP	0.33	0.47	0.48	0.67	0.48
	1	4	3	1	9
LAC	...	0.44	0.51	...	0.50
		4	12		16
SSA	0.40	0.45	0.63	...	0.44
	10	6	2		18
SAR	0.40	0.43	...	...	0.42
	2	3			5
DEV	...	...	...	0.76	0.76
				21	21
Total	0.39	0.45	0.52	0.72	0.54
	14	24	30	29	97

Note: MNA = Middle East and North Africa; ECA = Europe and Central Asia; EAP = East Asia and Pacific;
LAC = Latin America and the Caribbean; SSA = Sub-Saharan Africa; and DEV = developed countries.
... = no observations for that category.

The striking fact about Factor 6 is that all of the developing regions show roughly the same scores—when compared within income groups. Moreover, this factor is highly correlated with income, with all regions showing the same trend of increasing scores as income rises. Thus, the total regional differences appear to be a function of the number of countries in each income group, with those regions with more countries in higher income groups posting higher scores. With regards to the high income group, all high income countries in MENA, Europe and Central Asia, and East Asia and Pacific have lower scores than the developed regions average, suggesting that there is some room for improvement for these countries. The bottom line is that MENA is no better or no worse than the other regions.

Figure A.3 presents a listing of the scores for several countries on subfactor 6.2 (Are government regulations applied and enforced without improper influence?). As before, we see some variability, especially within the MENA upper-middle income group, as Jordan scores much higher than Tunisia.

Factors 7 and 8: Access to Civil and Criminal Justice

Factor 7 assess the accessibility to civil justice (its affordability, effectiveness, and impartiality), while Factor 8 measures the effectiveness of criminal justice (including the level of investigative capacity, impartiality, and the protection of the rights of the accused).

As with Factor 6, all regions show the same trend for both Factors 7 and 8: scores increase as income rises. For civil justice, MENA performs best among

Figure A.3 WJP Subfactor 6.2

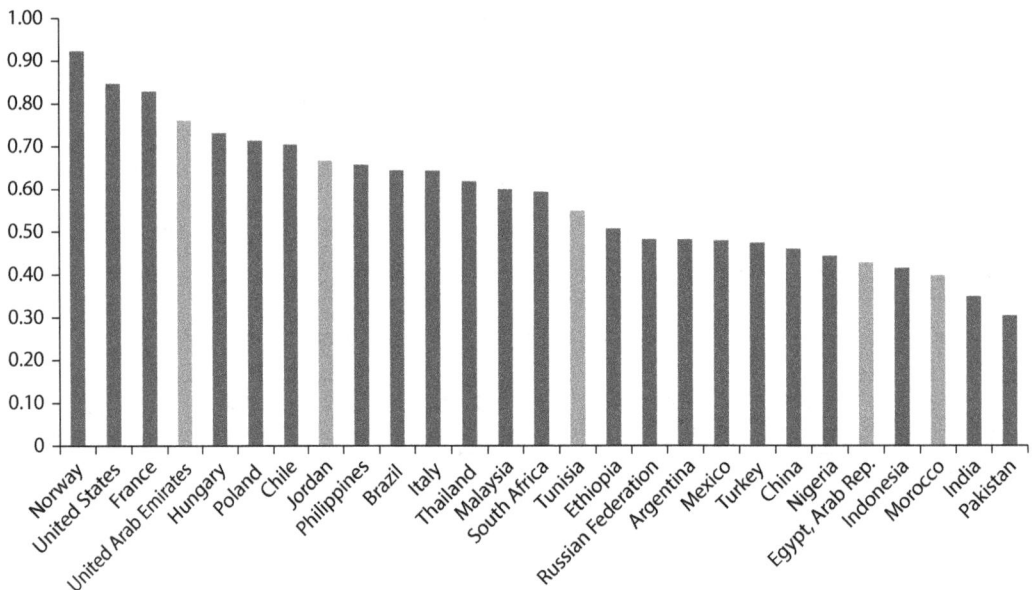

Table A.7 WJP Factor 7—Civil Justice

Region	Income				
	Low	Lower middle	Upper middle	High	Total
MNA	...	0.50	0.57	0.60	0.56
		2	4	1	7
ECA	0.46	0.51	0.54	0.61	0.55
	1	5	9	6	21
EAP	0.37	0.47	0.48	0.72	0.49
	1	4	3	1	9
LAC	...	0.43	0.51	...	0.49
		4	12		16
SSA	0.49	0.51	0.60	...	0.51
	10	6	2		18
SAR	0.38	0.45	...	...	0.42
	2	3			5
DEV	...	...	...	0.72	0.72
				21	21
Total	0.46	0.48	0.53	0.69	0.56
	14	24	30	29	97

Note: MNA = Middle East and North Africa; ECA = Europe and Central Asia; EAP = East Asia and Pacific;
LAC = Latin America and the Caribbean; SSA = Sub-Saharan Africa; and DEV = developed countries.
... = no observations for that category.

Table A.8 WJP Factor 8—Criminal Justice

Region	Income				
	Low	Lower middle	Upper middle	High	Total
MNA	...	0.40	0.50	0.75	0.50
		2	4	1	7
ECA	0.35	0.44	0.50	0.66	0.52
	1	5	9	6	21
EAP	0.40	0.50	0.58	0.76	0.54
	1	4	3	1	9
LAC	...	0.33	0.43	...	0.41
		4	12		16
SSA	0.43	0.38	0.61	...	0.43
	10	6	2		18
SAR	0.46	0.48	...	...	0.47
	2	3			5
DEV	...	...	...	0.74	0.74
				21	21
Total	0.43	0.42	0.49	0.73	0.53
	14	24	30	29	97

Note: MNA = Middle East and North Africa; ECA = Europe and Central Asia; EAP = East Asia and Pacific;
LAC = Latin America and the Caribbean; SSA = Sub-Saharan Africa; and DEV = developed countries.
... = no observations for that category.

Table A.9 WJP Rule of Law Summary Table

Factor	General trend	MENA trend
1. Limited Government	Scores improve with income	MENA scores on average—higher for the lower-middle income countries and lower for the high income countries.
2. Absence of Corruption	Scores improve with income, especially from upper-middle income to high income.	MENA scores on average—but slightly higher for the lower-middle income countries.
3. Order and Security	Scores similar for low, lower-middle, and upper-middle income countries. Big increase when moving from upper-middle income to high income.	Similar to ECA and EAP, MENA scores above average across all income groups.
4. Fundamental Rights	Scores improve with income	MENA scores the lowest among all regions and for each income group.
5. Open Government	Scores improve with income	Scores do not improve with income and—except for low income the Arab Republic of Egypt and Morocco—MENA scores the lowest among all regions.
6. Regulatory Enforcement	**Scores improve with income**	**MENA on average with other regions. No better or no worse than other regions by income groups.**
7. Civil Justice	Scores improve with income	MENA scores on average—slightly higher for the upper-middle income countries and lower for the high income countries.
8. Criminal Justice	Scores improve with income	MENA scores on average, higher than LAC and SSA, but lower than EAP.
General Rule-of-Law Index	**Scores improve with income**	**MENA scores on average with other developing regions for the low- and upper-middle income groups. It scores lower for the high income group.**

Source: Elaboration based on the World Justice Project's eight categories and general rule-of-law index.
Note: MNA = Middle East and North Africa; ECA = Europe and Central Asia; EAP = East Asia and Pacific; LAC = Latin America and the Caribbean; and SSA = Sub-Saharan Africa.

developing regions, reflecting the high average scores for lower-middle and upper-middle income countries, which are above the averages for their income groups. The United Arab Emirates is somewhat lower than the average but is on par with high income Europe and Central Asia. For criminal justice, MENA comes in on average for each income group.

Two exceptions exist, however: on order and security, several regions score high even at low income levels; and in relation to the absence of corruption, along a rising trend, there is a significant increase when moving from the upper-middle income countries to the high income countries. See Table A.9.

Summary

MENA scores higher than average with the Order and Security category (along with Europe and Central Asia and East Asia and Pacific) and lower than average with the more citizens-rights focused categories of Fundamental Rights and Open Government. For the rest, MENA scores roughly on average with other regions.

Accordingly, for the general rule-of-law index, MENA scores roughly on average as well.

More importantly, in the factor that is the primary focus of this study, regulatory enforcement, there is no significant difference between MENA and the other developing regions. As for the ancillary-to-enforcement Absence of Corruption factor, again MENA scores roughly on average by income category. In sum, with regards to regulatory enforcement, MENA performs no better and no worse than other regions.

Rules on Paper, Rules in Practice • http://dx.doi.org/10.1596/978-1-4648-0886-9

Environmental Benefits Statement

The World Bank Group is committed to reducing its environmental footprint. In support of this commitment, the Publishing and Knowledge Division leverages electronic publishing options and print-on-demand technology, which is located in regional hubs worldwide. Together, these initiatives enable print runs to be lowered and shipping distances decreased, resulting in reduced paper consumption, chemical use, greenhouse gas emissions, and waste.

The Publishing and Knowledge Division follows the recommended standards for paper use set by the Green Press Initiative. The majority of our books are printed on Forest Stewardship Council (FSC)–certified paper, with nearly all containing 50–100 percent recycled content. The recycled fiber in our book paper is either unbleached or bleached using totally chlorine-free (TCF), processed chlorine-free (PCF), or enhanced elemental chlorine-free (EECF) processes.

More information about the Bank's environmental philosophy can be found at http://www.worldbank.org/corporateresponsibility.